HELP KIDS SAY NO TO DRUGS AND DRINKING

Bob Schroeder

CompCare Publishers
Minneapolis, Minnesota

©1987 Alcoholism Council of Nebraska
All rights reserved.
Published in the United States
by CompCare Publishers,
a division of Comprehensive Care Corporation.

Schroeder, Bob, 1945-
    Help kids say no to drugs and drinking / Bob Schroeder.
        p.   cm.
    ISBN 0-89638-124-2 (pbk.) : $6.95
    1. Children—United States—Drug use.
2. Children—United States—Alcohol use.
3. Drug abuse—United States—Prevention.
4. Alcoholism—United States—Prevention.
5. Parenting—United States.   I. Title.
HV5824.C45S34   1987
649'.4—dc19   87-20997
                                                                        CIP

Cover design by Jeremy Gale

    Inquiries, orders, and catalog requests should be addressed to
    CompCare Publishers
    2415 Annapolis Lane
    Minneapolis, Minnesota 55441
    Call toll free 800/328-3330
    (Minnesota residents 612/559-4800)

6   5   4   3   2   1

92   91   90   89   88   87

This book is dedicated to my wife, Judy, my friend and mentor. To the kids—Chad, Emily, Erin, Jill, Matthew, Mike, and Sarah—for the richness, depth, and challenge they've added to my life. And to the many people who have played a part in my recovery from alcoholism.

Contents

Foreword

Bob Schroeder has compiled a series of homespun vignettes (he calls them essays) with a focus on cameo performances by members of his family. The stars are the author, his wife, and their seven children. The setting is middle America.

There are most important threads running through these glimpses into the life of Bob Schroeder's family. You learn about personal weaknesses and strengths, feelings, communication skills, parenting techniques, and the use of alcohol and other drugs, just for starters.

In my view, it is not a book to be read in one or two settings. These vignettes are most valuable when read one at a time. Reflecting on what you have read will bring you insights into dilemmas about the successes and failures you are experiencing. With these insights, you can become a better person—and just possibly a better parent.

This book is a journey through which few readers will pass untouched and unmoved. Bob Schroeder has written a valuable, entertaining, and thought-provoking work.

> James E. Kelsey, M.D., chairman of the board,
> National Council on Alcoholism

* * * * *

This book puts parents in the driver's seat. With care, commitment, consistency, communication, and common sense, parents can give their children some immunity to the devastating and contagious epidemic of drug use.

Bob Schroeder's essays suggest use of parents' most powerful tool—influence. A child as young as age four can feel this influence, continue to feel it at fourteen—and for a lifetime.

We should work together to change society so that our culture becomes a safer place. In the meantime, we are not helpless. Armed with the ideas and attitudes set forth in these essays, parents can be a strong protective influence for a drug-free lifestyle.

We do this by developing our knowledge, setting our standards, sharing with our children, and becoming adults our kids can look to for stability. The advice I most appreciate is that we laugh with our kids!

There is no known vaccine to protect a child from alcoholism/chemical dependency. Our best hope for immunization is protecting our children from drug *use*. Prevention of drug and alcohol problems may be the greatest gift we can give our children!

Regardless of your child's age, this book can be your guide. Its clarity and logic empower you to be the positive influence your children need in their lives.

> Mary Jacobson, charter member and past president, National Federation of Parents for Drug-Free Youth; former member of the National Institute on Drug Abuse (NIDA) Advisory Board

Introduction

It's a tough world out there, and it's taking its toll on our kids. They're dropping like flies: depression, suicide, school problems, trouble with the law, car accidents, emotional problems, and pregnancy. And the biggest problem of all—and contributor to so many of the other problems—is alcohol and other drugs.

I hear parents say, "Aw, let 'em have a little fun. What's the big deal? Kids will be kids. We were young once too. We sowed our wild oats and ended up just fine."

Well, maybe you did and maybe you didn't. But no matter. The world facing our kids today is much different and far tougher than the world we grew up in.

The pressures on our kids are tremendous. "Go ahead, have a little sex, smoke a little pot, drink some beer, steal a little money, ignore what your parents say. Pretend you're an adult in a world you're not nearly ready for."

So where do we start? How do we guide our kids through these scary times—the experiment-with-alcohol-and-drugs years?

We start at home, within our families. And we start early. We guide them through love, through example, through firm discipline, and through education.

In Alcoholics Anonymous meetings recovering alcoholics often say, "It's a simple Program, but it's not easy." They mean that the ideas on how to stay sober aren't hard to understand, but putting the ideas into practice can be hard work.

The same is true for parents trying to prevent alcohol and drug problems among their children. It's not hard to understand what to do, but doing it can be another matter.

The essays in this book will suggest what to do. But just reading them isn't enough—prevention means action. Prevention means commitment, setting examples, perhaps changing your own behavior as you help kids change theirs. It also means setting standards—saying no to kids, and doing what's best for them, in spite of what they, or others, might say or do or think.

Over time, little by little, we can become alcohol and drug abuse prevention experts. We can become as efficient in teaching kids how to avoid alcohol and drugs as we are already in teaching our kids to look both ways before crossing the street safely.

I hope that someday our world will be free of alcohol and drug problems. But we can't wait for someday. We need to start now, in our own homes, with our own kids.

The essays that follow were written by a parent struggling to bring up healthy alcohol/drug-free kids in a pro-alcohol/drug world.

May these suggestions point you in the right direction. The rest is up to you.

Bob Schroeder, executive director,
Alcoholism Council of Nebraska, Lincoln

1

Moments that trigger talk

There are times when we suddenly learn a great deal because of something we have seen or heard. We are open to learning because something has caught our attention.

A few weeks ago a house close to ours caught fire. A little boy had been playing with matches on the front porch. It was a spectacular fire, with flames shooting out into the street. Fortunately no one was hurt, although the house suffered thousands of dollars worth of damage. Our kids saw the whole thing. We were even the ones who called the fire department.

As we watched, we experienced a whole range of feelings—fear, excitement, and relief. It was an hour burned (excuse the pun) into the memory of every member of our family. Even today when someone says, "Remember the fire…," we all stop, pay attention, and listen carefully to what's being said.

My wife and I have been able to use this experience many times to discuss fire safety with our kids. We've talked about playing with matches, going to a safe place, and calling for help. The fire was indeed a trigger for a lot of learning by our kids.

As parents, we can look for similar opportunities to talk to our kids about alcohol and other drugs. We do this by watching for times when an alcohol- or drug-related "trigger" has caught our kids' attention, and then discussing it with them while they are interested. For instance, I was watching the TV show "Cheers" with a couple of the kids. Carla, a barmaid on the show who was pregnant, poured herself a beer. This bothered me, and I wanted to counteract this high-risk message the kids had just seen. I said, "Women who are pregnant shouldn't be drinking; the baby could get hurt. Whoever wrote the show must not know that." The comment was brief and did not require an answer from the kids.

1

Last fall at a university football game, some spectators behind us were drinking and got increasingly drunk as the game went on. It was obvious that my kids were very aware of the drinkers and were affected by their behavior. This was a "trigger," and all the way home from the game we talked about how we felt (afraid, disgusted, angry), what was unacceptable drinking, and how alcohol affects people. The kids—the youngest was only five—paid close attention.

A lot of other "triggers" have led to discussions about alcohol and drugs. Beer ads that feature athletes usually grab my boys' attention. During one ad, I asked them why they thought the slogan "Tastes great . . . less filling" was used. After a little thought one replied, "They say less filling so people will drink more, and then they'll sell more beer." The kids will never be hooked by that ad.

Parents are already prevention experts when it comes to other matters of health and well-being. We naturally help our kids with dental care, diet, and traffic safety. It's quite simple to add this new topic—alcohol and other drug use.

You can start talking about alcohol and drugs when your kids are young, often as early as age five. It's just a matter of looking for the "triggers" and then inserting the information you want them to have.

Make your comments short, especially for younger kids (their eyes start getting that glazed look after about twenty seconds). Don't lecture—just make a comment or ask a question. The kids will let you know if they want to keep talking about the subject.

A good way for parents to begin talking about alcohol and drugs is simply to share reactions with each other over dinner or while driving in the car. You'll be surprised how many little ears perk up, yet you've made no demands on the children to listen or reply.

Look for moments when you can talk to your kids about alcohol and other drugs. You'll be amazed at just how many of these "trigger" opportunities there are!

Prevention principle: Look for situations in which you can share with your kids your own standards of drug and alcohol use (or non-use). Temper the high-risk messages they see around them with timely conversations that impart low-risk information. Even a five-year-old can benefit from hearing parental standards expressed.

2

A chip off the old block

The earliest memory I have of my grandfather is of him sneaking a big slug of whiskey when Grandma wasn't looking.

I was three or four at the time, and we'd go into the upstairs bathroom in his home. There was a clothes chute in the corner; you opened the lid, dropped in your dirty clothes, and they fell all the way to the basement. Grandpa had a string on a nail inside the chute and hanging on the end of the string, hidden partway down, was a bottle of whiskey.

Several times a day we'd go up, and Grandpa would reach down into the clothes chute, pull the bottle up by the string, and take a big drink. Grandma never did find our hiding place. Although Grandpa eventually quit drinking a few years before he died, I suspect that some of his insides finally gave out from years of heavy drinking.

More than ten years have passed now since I began my own recovery from alcoholism. During these years I've thought a lot and learned a lot about this illness, what it's like, and who seems to get it. This is some of what I've put together so far:

- Anyone who drinks or uses drugs runs the risk of getting hooked.

- The more you use, the greater the risk.

- The amount of drinking necessary to trigger alcoholism seems to vary greatly from person to person.

- Nobody thinks it can happen to him or her.

- Most people know very little about alcoholism, especially when they make their initial drinking choices.

5

- Nobody ever plans to become alcoholic or chemically dependent, and one's physical make-up seems to have a great deal to do with whether or not alcoholism will develop.

Here's where Grandpa fits back into the story. People who have relatives, especially parents or grandparents, with alcohol problems are at much higher risk for becoming alcoholic themselves. The more alcoholism in the family, the greater the risk seems to be.

While not all alcoholic people have alcoholic relatives, about half do. Many experts believe that some sort of physical susceptibility to alcohol is passed from parent to child. In other words, some people are born with bodies that react to alcohol differently, and in such a way that dependency on alcohol results very easily. We think the same thing may be true for other drugs.

And so, while it appears that *anyone* can become hooked, some people become dependent after drinking far less than others. People with alcoholism in their family history are particularly vulnerable.

I didn't realize there was alcoholism in my family. As in the case of many alcoholic families who live by the don't-mention-the-alcohol-problem rule, nobody talked about it while I was growing up. As a result, when I began to drink, I did so without any guidelines and ignorant of the fact that I was at high risk for becoming dependent. I'll never know if having more guidance and information about my family history would have made a difference. Perhaps my initial choices about drinking would have been different.

Alcoholism is one of many illnesses that runs in families. I believe that kids have a right to be taught about any illness they may be especially susceptible to. In our family we frequently talk about this illness. Our kids know they are at high risk for alcoholism and we are encouraging them to make abstinence a lifelong choice because of that fact.

Prevention principle: If there is alcoholism in the family, don't hide it from your children. Let them know that they may be particularly susceptible to it–and encourage them to make the safe choice of lifelong abstinence.

Bathroom

Tube
Sike
floor Sweep to a Shake the rug
toylet
Cuvert
Take out the girbege
Stanen the towes
Take wet wosclofs tobasmet
Choeck The Mregccn

3

Matthew's bathroom

One of the most effective tools for parents to use in preventing alcohol and drug use by their kids is to set specific expectations. That means letting your kids know exactly what you expect from them when it comes to the use of alcohol and drugs. Kids whose parents have communicated clear, firm expectations of abstinence along with set consequences for using are much more likely to honor those expectations and remain alcohol- and drug-free.

Let me give you an example of how setting specific expectations has worked in our home. This past summer vacation we had seven kids at home, including a newborn. As you might guess, with that many kids, we have to run the household like a boot camp or chaos will result. This means that each kid (except baby Emily) has specific household chores to perform.

Matthew, a second grader, through the luck of the draw, pulled bathroom cleanup.

His cleanup was a disaster. We had not given him specific instructions on what to do and how to do it. He would be either going from task to task feeling overwhelmed or sitting on the edge of the tub not knowing what to do next. In order to finish his job, pass inspection, and get out to play, he would constantly be asking my wife, Judy, for help.

After a couple of days, Judy had had enough. She sat down with Matthew and the two of them set specific expectations for how the bathroom was to be cleaned. What resulted was a list of things to be done, and the order in which to do them.

Now he knows to start by cleaning the "tube" and "sike." He has to "stanen the towes" on the towel rack and make sure the wet "wosclafs" get to the "basment." When he has "chaecked" the "mreaer" to make sure it's clean, he's finished and can go play.

He's much happier now that he knows exactly what's expected of him. And, besides, the bathroom gets cleaned.

Preparing our children for a life without alcohol or drug problems is no simple task. I believe we can help our kids do this through combinations of parental modeling, teaching, and setting limits. And even then there are no guarantees—the choice is ultimately their own. However, if I were to pick one key—one thing for every parent to do—it would be to sit down and set expectations with kids as they enter the dangerous years of exposure to alcohol and drugs.

Guidelines for setting expectations on alcohol and drug use for kids are quite simple:

- Have clear in your mind exactly what you expect (we recommend no use of illegal drugs ever, and no use of alcohol until young people are of legal age).

- Sit down with your kids and tell them exactly what you expect and why.

- List the consequences that will occur if they do not honor your expectations (they should be immediate and important to your child).

- Be prepared to follow through.

Don't miss the chance to use this most helpful tool—it works!

Prevention principle: State clearly exactly what you expect from your children, whether it has to do with daily tasks or with the use of alcohol and other drugs. Parents who expect abstinence—who have established standards of non-use, along with a predictable set of consequences if these expectations are not met—are more likely to avoid the problems and heartaches that teenage drinking and drug-using can bring.

4

Movies and messages

Our kids are bombarded by messages that tell them that drinking or using drugs is glamorous, humorous, harmless, and mature. They get it from all sides: peers, advertisements, TV shows, rock music, and movies.

I saw a movie a while back that really made me angry. I don't think it tells the truth to people. The film was *The Breakfast Club*.

It's about a group of high school kids who, because they broke school rules, have to spend all day Saturday at school. As we might expect, the group includes a star athlete, a neurotic, a drugger, a pretty little rich girl, and a brain (homely, of course). The only adult in the movie, a male teacher assigned to supervise, is—stereotyped for guaranteed youth appeal—a first-class jerk, cruel, unfeeling, narcissistic, and dull.

For the first part of the day, the kids are at each other's throats. They trade cruel comments, almost come to blows, are isolated from each other and obviously lonely. We know these kids are hurting inside (because of how their rotten parents have treated them) but they just can't express their feelings to one another. It looks as if it's going to be a long day for them.

And then something happens. Magic. The answer. They start smoking marijuana. Soon the barriers between them begin to disappear. They get honest with each other and talk about the pain in their lives. They become filled with insight and truth about life. They help each other. They bond with each other. They understand each other. The druggie gets the little rich girl, and the adult teacher continues to make a fool of himself.

In my opinion, the message was clear: there's nothing wrong with smoking pot. In fact, it's not only fun, it's helpful. It makes you real, brings you close to people. It's good for the mind and spirit.

13

And that's what makes me angry: what I perceive as the lie. Drugs don't solve people's problems; they create them. Drugs don't bring people close together; drugs push people apart. Drug use doesn't make kids honest; it makes kids lie and steal and violate their values. Drugs don't help kids feel; drugs make kids unfeeling zombies. Kids who depend on drugs to build relationships have built relationships on sand.

If you want to see what smoking pot can really do, spend a couple of hours in a drug/alcohol treatment program for young people and look at the new kids in treatment. You will see some of the loneliest, most isolated people on the face of the earth. You will see young people numbed from their feelings, out of touch with reality, and with little or no ability to relate successfully with other people.

I hate movies that lie to kids. Kids start believing that stuff. And this example is not an isolated instance; examples are everywhere. The medium or the actors or the words may be different. But the message is the same: drug-taking is only fun—it won't hurt you. A lie. It will.

There has been some talk, from a group of entertainment figures, about trying to get a substance abuse (SA) sub-rating for movies to tell moviegoers (and parents) about inappropriate portrayals of alcohol and other drugs. I wholeheartedly support this idea. I hope you do too.

In the meantime, be conscious of the messages your kids are receiving. And don't be afraid to step in and say no to your kids when it comes to what they watch, what they hear, and what they do.

Prevention principle: Be aware of the prevalence of false messages that kids are getting about drinking and drug use. The idea that "drinking or taking drugs is okay" may be found even in movies and TV shows that have won popular and critical acclaim. Parents should be prepared to counteract these untruths with truths.

5

Erin's tantrum

One very good technique that parents can use to help their kids stay away from alcohol and drugs is to set specific expectations for kids, backed up by logical consequences.

Last night when I got home from work, Erin, a second grader, was in her swimming suit waiting for me. "The neighbors invited me to their pool! Can I go? Can I? Can I?"

Just as I was about to say okay, her older sister, Sarah, who had been babysitting that afternoon, said, "I think you should know that Erin has been a brat today. She knew she couldn't go swimming until you came home, but she kept trying to get me to let her go. She threw temper tantrums all afternoon."

Erin's face fell. She knew she had been caught. Giving older sisters a hard time when they are babysitting is a serious offense in our family. I knew right away what her consequence would be. She would not go swimming. It was a good punishment because it was immediate, tied directly to her rotten behavior, and important to her.

Naturally she tried to change my mind. "Maybe a good punishment would be for me to go to bed an hour early," she said. "Or maybe I should have to do the supper dishes all by myself." I stuck to my decision, however, even though I knew she was very disappointed.

Later that evening we talked about what had happened. Yes, she said, she had really hoped I would choose a different punishment for her. Not going swimming was the one that really got her. But she also agreed that it was good in the sense that she lost something important because of her tantrum and she'll think twice before she throws another one.

The incident illustrates an important prevention principle. Our expectation is that she behave for her babysitter, and she knows that. She did not, so she was given a logical consequence, and one that was effective. I hope that now she has learned that taking advantage of babysitters will result in great personal loss to her and she will not do it again.

This same idea applies well to behavior related to alcohol and drugs. If you have told your kids they are not to use, but they use anyway and then are given meaningless consequences (or none at all), what's to stop them from doing it again?

A recent study done in Minnesota showed that the biggest factor in reduced alcohol and drug use among kids is the child's perception that parents will be very concerned if they discover their child has been drinking or using drugs. A strong indication of parental concern is establishing and following through with consequences.

Let your kids know ahead of time what will happen to them if they use mind-altering chemicals. In deciding on consequences, you should make sure that they are reasonable, important to the child, and related to the event. And once you've made your decision, be prepared to carry it through.

An acquaintance of mine has a younger brother who bought an old car and then drove home one Saturday night after he had been drinking. Early the next morning, his dad got him out of bed, hangover and all, and had him drive the car out behind the barn. The young man then had to jack up the car, put blocks underneath it, and then take off all four tires. The tires were locked away, the car sat on the blocks all summer, and the young man got the message: "Around this house, drinking and driving is a serious offense."

Now there was an effective consequence!

Prevention principle: Consequences for breaking any rule should be immediate, related to the infringement, and important to the child. This principle applied to alcohol or drug use becomes a powerful deterrent.

6

72 in a 55 zone

Parents have a great deal of influence in determining what kids do, how kids think, and how kids behave both during childhood and when they become adults.

Last Saturday I was driving home on the Interstate from a trip out of town with two of my kids. I looked in my rearview mirror and saw a State Patrol car right on my tail with its red lights on. It seemed to have come out of nowhere. The officer politely, but curtly, informed me that I had been clocked at 72 miles per hour and the speed limit was 55. He gave me a ticket for fifty dollars.

Of course the kids couldn't wait to get home to tell everybody. It was the big news on the block. I also knew that the look my wife would give me would hurt almost as much as the loss of fifty bucks.

I frequently make this particular trip between cities, and, to be honest, I usually speed. My wife has been after me to drive the speed limit. "Not only," she says, "do you increase the risk of getting hurt, you are also modeling a bad behavior. Because you do it, you're telling the kids it's okay. You're raising a pack of future speeders. Is that what you want?"

Of course not, but old habits are hard to change. I know she's right, and I'll work on it. Anyway, she's glad I got the ticket and hopes that fifty bucks out of my pocket will give me the incentive to change my behavior.

Now the same idea—modeling—applies to alcohol and drug use. Every time you get intoxicated or use drugs, you're saying to your kids: this is an okay way to live. Every time you come home after a tough day at work and relax with a few drinks, you're saying to your kids: this is a good way to cope.

If you drink at most of your activities or social gatherings, you're saying to your children that drinking is a necessary part of having fun. If you drink and drive...well, I'm sure you get the point.

Here, again, is another place where prevention can get tough and be a lot of work. We (parents) may have to change how we do some things. Change is rarely easy. Driving the speed limit is going to be hard for me to do, but I'm going to start. I urge you to examine your drinking and drug-use behavior. If you're setting an unhealthy or high-risk example, begin to change it.

Your kids will notice.

Prevention principle: When it comes to drinking and drug use, model the kind of behavior that you'd like your kids to follow. In this area of chemical use, all the verbal decrees and guidelines you may give your children are never as effective as your setting an example for them—living your convictions.

7

Players, spectators...and drinking

This essay is probably going to irritate a few people. You might think that I'm just nitpicking. Maybe so—but read on, and you be the judge.

I think tournament competitions in sports are a great idea—both as an opportunity for athletes to compete and as a chance for spectators to watch many fine amateur athletes in action. I was a spectator at the statewide games held in our town recently and had been looking forward to them for months.

I watched the softball competition and was there at the finals of the men's slow-pitch tournament. It was exciting to see. The semi-final game had been hard fought and was decided by only one run.

What I noticed as much as the games, however, was how much drinking was going on. I would estimate that about half the spectators were drinking. Between games, players would drink beer and then go play again. Coolers full of beer were everywhere. I didn't see a single can of pop.

One game was repeatedly marred by arguing and complaining over umpires' calls. One player was ejected from the game and others nearly were. I believe the drinking contributed to the game almost getting out of hand.

The athletes talked about how they were going to "get smashed tonight" to celebrate. Players who had been drinking got behind the wheels of their cars after the game and drove off, apparently without thought of the risk (many had to drive long distances).

The guy who seemed to be in charge walked around during the games drinking beer and wearing a T-shirt that said "University of Budweiser" on the front. Although he didn't have a beer in his hand as he presented the medals to the players, he did have a cigarette hanging out of his mouth.

I know that, because of my own background and work experience, I am very sensitive to this kind of thing. I wonder if I was the only person who noticed. Maybe others felt the way I did, and went home a little bit bothered. But maybe not; drinking is so ingrained in our society that nobody seems to notice when alcohol use seems to permeate an event.

I called the city parks and recreation department on the morning after the games and a staff member there confirmed my hunch that it is against the law to drink at this ball park. But nobody seemed to care.

I dug through my newspapers and found what the governor had said at the opening ceremony of the amateur games: that these statewide games were to serve two main purposes—to showcase the abilities of athletes and "to remind us all of the importance of a healthy lifestyle." Demonstration of athletes' abilities—yes. An example of a healthy lifestyle—no.

Maybe it's because people think, "Oh well, it's only beer, and beer won't hurt you." What if everyone had been drinking hard stuff instead? I wonder what the reaction would have been if the spectators and ballplayers had pulled half-pints of vodka from their back pockets and taken big slugs every so often.

So many of us think of beer as a harmless drink and ignore evidence that beer drinkers typically get drunker, are more likely to drive after drinking, and tend to consider driving while intoxicated as less serious than those who prefer wine or distilled spirits.

·I'm not against anyone's right to drink. But there's a time and a place for drinking, and athletic events provide neither. I try to teach my kids that sports and drinking don't mix and that you don't have to drink to have a good time. I thought the state games would be a great example of both of these tenets. Unfortunately, they were not.

I'm probably fighting an uphill battle here. I don't expect a lot of people to agree with what I'm saying, or that many changes will be made. As I said, drinking is so much a part of our lives.

But I can write my concerns in a letter to the organizers of athletic events like this one, and you never know what might happen. Maybe if others do the same thing, someday games and sports competitions may come a little closer to that demonstration of "healthy lifestyles" the governor talked about.

Prevention principle: Develop an awareness of just how often sports events and drinking—especially beer-drinking—are paired. (Or, for that matter, count the number of beer commercials when games are televised!) It's almost inevitable that your children will pick up sports-and-alcohol-are-okay, sports-and-alcohol-are-fun messages. When they do, be sure you counteract these messages with some of your own. And keep letting whoever's in charge know how you feel about the emphasis on drinking at sports events.

8

Taming the TV monster

It happened one too many times. I walked in the front door and there they were, six kids lying on the living room floor staring at some show on TV. Nobody seemed to notice that I had just come home from another hard day at work. Nobody seemed to care either. They just had blank looks on their faces. I picked my way through the bodies and had an emergency meeting with my wife.

Yes, she had noticed it too. We made a decision right there and then. We would take control of the television and severely limit the time it was on.

The next day we had a family meeting to explain the new rules. Each person could choose one hour of TV per week. No more. On Sundays kids were to pick the shows they wanted to watch during the following week. All shows had to be approved by parents. They could watch each other's shows. Occasionally a special movie (*The Wizard of Oz*, for example) would be thrown in by us as a bonus. The rest of the time the television was to be off. Period.

The kids hit the roof, every last one of them. We were taking away a God-given right. It was in the Constitution. They considered hiring a lawyer. No loving parent would ever do this. We held firm, however, and stuck by our decision. For the last couple of months the TV has been on about six to eight hours a week, down from thirty to thirty-five.

At dinner one night this week I took a poll and asked a few questions. I asked, "Do any of you kids like the rule of one hour of TV per week?" Their replies shocked me. Three of them actually said they liked the rule, and the other three only griped mildly!

Then I asked why they liked the rule—and why the other three didn't hate it so much anymore. Some of their replies were:

"You don't even seem to miss it after a while."

"It seems like we get to do a lot more stuff together."

"We get to spend more time with you and Mom."

Now what does turning the television off have to do with preventing alcohol and drug problems among kids? I would suggest it contributes in at least three ways:

- The average kid sees thousands of beer ads and high-risk drinking scenes on TV. If you reduce TV watching by 75 percent, you cut out exposure to ads by 75 percent also. That has to help.

- The children have had to learn new ways of participating in activities and involvement with each other rather than being passively entertained by TV. They have increased their interpersonal skills and may be learning alternative activities to alcohol and drug use.

- With the TV off, parents will probably spend more "quality time" with their kids. Most experts contend that a close parent-child relationship lowers the likelihood of future alcohol and drug problems in kids.

A couple of words of caution to parents who may consider turning off the TV. First, you'll lose your built-in babysitter. You'll be more involved with your kids, and that takes time. Second, you'll lose *your* TV time too. But I would guess that, after a few days of confusion, irritability, and withdrawal, you'll probably like it off. I do.

Prevention principle: By limiting the amount of television your kids watch, and by approving the programs, you can reduce the number of high-risk messages about drinking that they see, help them find new and constructive ways to use their time and energy, and give them the chance to get to know each other—and their parents—better.

9

Those leather high-tops

Most parents are concerned about the negative effects of peer pressure on their kids, especially when it comes to alcohol and drugs. Pressure from friends and acquaintances is often the reason why young people begin to use.

There are many ways we can help our kids resist peer pressure. One I'd suggest is teaching them that this kind of pressure influences everyone, including parents. By talking about how we feel and react to peer pressure, we're saying, "We're in this together; peer pressure isn't just a kid problem." This makes it more likely that kids will talk to us about pressure from their friends and will be open to receiving help from us.

I like to talk about times I did great in resisting pressure, but I also think it's important to give my kids examples of times I "buckled under" and wish I hadn't. We still laugh about one of those times.

One Saturday morning my sixth-grade son was playing in the season's first YMCA basketball game. As I walked into the gym, I noticed something that horrified me: Chad was the only boy without expensive leather high-top basketball shoes.

The contrast with the other kids' shoes was awful to me. His were an off-brand, low-cut, and canvas. There was nothing wrong with them, except that they were different. Therefore *he* was different, and I wanted him to be just like his teammates. As he raced up and down the court, it wasn't his playing I noticed; it was his shoes.

The game was a good one. Chad played well, and his team won. And he couldn't have cared less about his "off-brand" canvas shoes. But not me: I was obsessed for the rest of the weekend with his "need" to get leather high-top shoes. But there was the reality of the thirty-to-fifty-dollar price tag.

33

On Monday I was still brooding when Janet, our work-student, came into the office. My eyes immediately were drawn to her feet. There they were—the most beautiful pair of broken-in leather high-top shoes I'd ever seen. Her feet looked about the same size as Chad's, and I knew that I had to get those shoes!

Three days later, I finally persuaded Janet to sell me the shoes for fifteen dollars, and before the next game I gave them to Chad. They were a little big, but with extra socks finally he could look just like the other kids.

A few days went by before I realized what I had done—caved in to pressure to conform. What made it worse was that no one had said a word to me. The pressure was completely internal. Later another thought hit me: if a "mature," "experienced" adult can so easily succumb to pressure to be like everyone else, it must be very, very difficult for young people to resist pressure from their friends, especially when it comes to using alcohol and drugs.

Two weeks passed before I told my wife what I'd done. She's still shaking her head.

Here's what I learned:

- The need to be like others is powerful–even to the point of doing things you later can't believe you did.

- Becoming an adult doesn't mean the pressure suddenly goes away.

- The pressure to be like others can be internal—the only voice that said "get leather high-tops" came from inside my head.

The incident has been useful in talking to my kids because it showed them that pressure to conform is a problem that everybody faces, not just kids. Laughing with and at me made them comfortable enough to talk about times when they faced pressure from their friends. And it was natural and easy to shift to talking about the pressure they will face to use alcohol and drugs.

This was one of the times I wish I'd done better. But I also share with my kids times when I resisted pressure even though it was scary to do so. I let them know that I like myself better for resisting.

Make peer pressure something that's easy to talk about in your home.

Prevention principle: Find ways to talk with your children about peer pressure as a lifelong issue, not just a young people's problem. Use yourself as an example (what adult has not succumbed now and then to pressure to "be like everybody else"?). Being open about this very human vulnerability may prompt children, in turn, to be open about situations in which they are pressured by other kids to use alcohol and drugs.

10

When the tooth fairy is tardy

Although I would have a hard time proving it, I believe that one of
the reasons kids use alcohol and drugs is to escape. If a child
doesn't learn that life is not always fun, then drinking or using
drugs can become very attractive when things don't go right, when
emotional pain occurs, or when life is just kind of boring.

If parents do not let their children experience boredom, pain, and
disappointment, the kids may be unprepared for the hard knocks—
and the minor disappointments—life will give them.

I have a hard time letting my kids experience any unhappiness
or disappointment. I want them to be happy all the time. Let me
give you my latest example:

Last Saturday morning my second-grade son, Matthew, lost a
tooth. He showed it to me and said, "Yay! The tooth fairy comes
tonight." (Translation: "I get fifty cents to spend on candy tomorrow
morning.") I filed a mental note—tonight after he goes to sleep, the
tooth fairy must visit.

For the rest of the day I knocked myself out for kids. I held Little
League baseball practice in the morning, took the children
swimming all afternoon, grilled hot dogs and hamburgers for them
at suppertime, and finally organized a "T-ball" game for every little
kid in the neighborhood.

By 9:30 P.M. I was ready to drop. It was all I could do just to lie
in front of the TV and stare. I was beat and ready for bed.

Then I remembered I had to play tooth fairy. That meant I had to
stay awake until Matthew went to sleep and then sneak into his
room and make the switch.

Well, he didn't go to sleep for almost two hours. By the time he
finally fell asleep I was ready to remove the rest of his teeth. About
midnight, two hours past my normal bedtime, I finally fell into bed,

37

the switch completed.

Over the next couple of days, as I talked about this little incident with some friends, a couple of things became clear. First of all, I tend to go to great lengths to protect my kids from any little disappointment. Yet, if the tooth fairy hadn't visited that night, Matthew probably would have been disappointed for about a minute and then not thought about it again all day.

I had given most of my day to kids, yet I felt guilty. What I should have done was go to bed when I was tired. The tooth fairy could have visited some other time. I could have simply told Matthew, "The tooth fairy doesn't work weekends," and let it go at that.

Now I'm quite sure that this incident is not going to be the determining factor in whether Matthew gets into alcohol or drugs. But if I continue to break my back to protect him from every little disappointment in life, I'm cheating him—handicapping him. He won't learn how to deal with disappointment, part of the ups and downs of living.

And perhaps one of the consequences of the inability of young people to cope with life's disappointments and pain is the use of alcohol and drugs to escape.

Prevention principle: If you find that you continually go to great lengths to protect kids from life's small—and large—disappointments, you may be keeping them from learning how to cope with living. And without the skills or experience for coping with life's darker moments, they may try to numb their hurts with alcohol and other drugs.

11

A family in pain

This little story is about a young teenager who got involved with alcohol and drugs and how it affected his family.

The first sign of trouble was the discovery of a small pipe in a drawer in his room. He denied that he used it to smoke pot. That was more than three years ago. The story is still not over.

Mary (not her real name), the mother of this teenager, said she'd be glad to talk to me. She hopes that letting other parents know what happened in her family might help them avoid some of the pain she went through.

This is the kind of family that you wouldn't expect to have problems: loving parents who spend time with their children; father a well-respected professional in the community; close involvement with the church; a family-centered way of life.

But the problems happened. And the symptoms were pretty typical. Money started disappearing from around the house. The teenager started running around with a different and older group of kids. "They just looked like the wrong kind of kids," Mary said.

Then, she reported, the mood changes began. Much of the time he was hostile and angry. Sometimes he was mellow and calm, especially when he came home at night, but often in the morning he would be angry again. His brothers and sisters were handy targets and took a lot of the verbal abuse he frequently dished out.

He began to skip school and avoided the family as much as possible. His grades in school dropped. When he drove the family sedan he left beer cans in it. And finally one night he totaled the car.

The whole mess got to be a game of sorts. Catch me if you can, but if you do I'll deny it. And then I'll get very angry and say you just don't trust me. Then you'll feel guilty.

"We never really saw him obviously high or intoxicated. No smell

41

of alcohol or pot, red eyes, or any of that." But the parents knew just the same.

As you might imagine, living with this kind of problem pushes a family to the limits. The parents did the very best they could. They tried to keep him home and set curfew limits, but he'd make life miserable for everybody in the family or he'd just up and leave. They tried to be gentle and understanding. They tried confronting him, setting strict limits. They tried to ignore the problem. Nothing seemed to help.

"I didn't know what to do, whom to turn to, whom to talk to," she said. "We were all alone. You tend to deny the problem on the outside, but inside you know it's there—all the time.

"When I found the pipe in the drawer, I was surprised and heartsick. I went through a time when I felt I was a failure as a mother. Our family life became a living hell."

Mary has found that many other families experience the same problem. "Since I've begun sharing with others, I find it's happening everywhere. But so many families keep it a secret and try to handle it by themselves. That's the wrong thing to do.

"They need to talk about it. You have to swallow your pride; you can't let it get in the way. Face it, you're not in control anymore. You need help with so many questions. Is this normal behavior for a teenager? Is he crazy? Am I crazy?"

One Sunday night last fall the crisis came. The young man was offered help a final time, and he once more denied that he had a problem. The family had to protect itself—he doesn't live at home anymore. And that's painful to his mother. The whole thing has been a strain on the family—and the marriage. But they're all hanging in there.

The boy says he's been drug-free for some months now. Mary desperately hopes so. But she's standing firm. "You don't come home until you've changed." It seems right—but so hard to do.

If you are concerned that your son or daughter may be involved with drugs and alcohol, take action. If you have trusted friends who will support you and your child, share the problem with them.

But then go further. Contact your local parents' group (your school system may have support groups for parents of drug-abusing young people), your child's school counselor or the very best chemical dependency youth counselor available, or your pastor. Or call the nearest Council on Alcoholism. The problem won't go away by ignoring it.

Prevention principle: Counselors who deal with youth and alcohol and drug problems seem to agree: one of the most powerful deterrants for kids' getting help is parents' natural denial that there is a problem. Conversely, one of the most powerful "prevention" strategies is early intervention—following up on your suspicions, setting limits and consequences, getting appropriate help for a child *before* more serious problems occur, and, if a child refuses help, practicing tough love. This may mean not allowing your child to live at home if he or she is drinking or using.

12

Rehearsals and refusals

One of the "hottest" and most helpful tools in the field of prevention right now is refusal skills.

Simply put, refusal skills give kids the ability to say no to peers when offered alcohol or other drugs.

I used to be an easy mark for people trying to sell stuff over the phone. I'd hem and haw and have a hard time saying no.

I finally got disgusted with myself and began to practice saying no ahead of time to phone solicitors. Now my response is automatic. As soon as I discover that I'm getting a sales pitch on the phone, I say politely but firmly, "No, thank you, I'm not interested." If the voice on the other end goes on, I say, "No, thank you, I'm not interested—good-bye." And then I hang up.

This little tactic saves me time, frustration, and, very likely, money. The key to my refusal success is simple: I think beforehand about what the request might be, rehearse the situation, and know exactly what I'm going to say.

We can teach the same refusal skills to our kids. We've talked about sitting down with our kids and setting expectations ("at this point in your life your mother and I expect you to abstain") and consequences ("if you don't follow this rule, you'll be grounded"). The next step is to teach them how to say no.

Refusal skills should be taught as a youngster enters the junior high years (normally the first time that alcohol and drugs will be offered) and again as the young person enters high school (a time of increased pressure to use and to ride with drinking drivers). They should also be rehearsed for specific occasions—a party or an out-of-town ball game, for example.

Here's how to do it. First, sit down with your children and let them know that soon they may be faced with the need to turn down alcohol or drugs. Tell them you want to help them be prepared for that time. Review your expectations and then set up a simulated situation:

"Let's say you're at the party Friday night, and this guy you really like—Bill, we'll call him—comes over to you with a beer in his hand and says, 'Here, Jill, have a drink.'"

Ask your child what she would do in this situation and have her practice turning down the drink. Then have your child practice again, this time with you (in the role of "Bill") applying more pressure: "What's the matter—are you chicken?" Help your child come up with responses that are clear, simple, and dignifying.

If your child practices beforehand, there is a good chance that the previously rehearsed words will be used in an actual drug/alcohol-use situation and your child will be able to resist the pressure to use, thereby honoring your expectations. Practicing the actual words ahead of time is important.

A few suggestions that might help:

- Offer yourself as a scapegoat. "No thanks, my dad would kill me."

- Encourage your child to go with a buddy who also agrees not to use, and to talk beforehand about what they'll say. Having some support will help.

- Suggest words of postponement. "Not now, maybe later." "Not tonight, thanks."

- Let your kids know that sometimes the pressure may get tough. They just might have to say a simple "no," clearly and firmly, and walk away. If this happens, give them a good deal of support and reinforcement at home for having the courage to say no.

- Use examples of your own to show how you have used refusal skills. By doing this, you emphasize that it's not just a "kid issue" and you avoid making it a "you don't trust me" issue.

Teach your kids how to say no. They have a right to be prepared.

Prevention principle: Refusals are easier with rehearsals. Teach kids, from junior high school ages on up, how to say no to alcohol and other drugs when they are offered. Set up practice situations—including exactly what to say—so that refusing drugs and alcoholic drinks becomes automatic for your kids, even under pressure from peers.

13

Fears that prevent prevention

My friend, a counselor and softball teammate, called me this morning. "What time's the game on Saturday. I really like your column so far and, by the way, when are you going to write a column on fear?"

"What do you mean?" I asked.

"Fear," he said. "I work with parents all the time. They don't talk to their kids about alcohol and drugs because they're afraid. Hasn't that ever happened to you?"

Oh, yeah. I forget about that. Sarah's prom night for instance. I had been working with groups of parents for over a year at the time, teaching a prevention course.

"Always know where your kids are, whom they're with, what they're doing, when they'll be home."

"Make it clear to your kids and their friends that you expect no drinking or drugs."

"Get to know the parents of your kids' friends. Don't be afraid to call them."

Then came our turn. Sarah was going to the prom, a night notorious for drinking and driving. Her group was driving to another town fifty miles away for dinner and then back for the dance. My wife came to me: "Well, Mr. Prevention, it's prom night and time to practice what we preach. We need to talk to Sarah, talk to her date who will be driving, and call the parents of the kids she's going with."

I knew what would happen. Sarah would see me as a meddling parent who didn't trust her and she would die from embarrassment. Her date would think I was a jerk and take it out on Sarah all evening. The other parents would think I was overcontrolling, overreacting, and implying that their kids were rascals.

49

Nevertheless it had to be done, and I did what any concerned father would do: I conned my wife into doing it.

And that's what she did. In spite of being afraid of what they would think, she talked to Sarah, her date, and the parents. It worked out fine. The other parents were glad she called, and had had the same concern. Sarah was relieved that the issue was dealt with up front; she didn't have to be the bad guy if the others wanted to drink. I think even her date appreciated the directness and honesty. The evening went well.

My wife had good feelings from doing what she knew was right in spite of being afraid. I was left with the unpleasant knowledge that it's easy to chicken out when prevention gets a little tough.

I guess there are a lot of reasons why we're afraid to talk to our kids, as well as other kids and parents, about alcohol and drugs.

For me, a big reason is my concern about what people will think of me. For other parents, it might be not knowing what to say or when to say it, or maybe saying the wrong thing altogether. Maybe we think that if we say the wrong thing, our kids might do the opposite of what we want. Whatever the reasons, too often we (I) say nothing.

Parenting is the toughest job I know of and the pay is lousy. We're always walking that fine line between "when do I need to let go of my children" and "when do I need to step in." Talking with kids about alcohol and drugs is pretty easy when they're small. It gets a lot tougher when they enter the teens. A few suggestions:

- If your gut feeling tells you that you had better do some talking or calling or checking things out, trust your feeling.

- If you don't know what to say or do, go find out. Take a good prevention course for parents or join a parents' group.

- Be honest about your feelings. You might start out by saying something like "It's scary for me to call you, but…" or "I'm afraid you might get angry, but I need to say this anyway…"

- Do it in spite of being afraid. That's what I'll do next time, and I'll bet I'll be glad I did.

- Start a network of the parents of your kids' friends—and set specific guidelines about alcohol and drugs. There's strength in numbers.

50

Prevention principle: Don't be afraid to check out your teenager's plans with the teens involved, and with other parents—to set limits in advance of an event or situation. How many parents who were afraid to do this ahead-of-time checking have spent prom nights in a state of sleepless anxiety?

14

Drinking and 'minor' hurts

It's important that parents teach their kids that there is a bad side to alcohol. Especially since advertising, TV, and movies rarely show the negatives. People *do* get hurt frequently by another's drinking, often in subtle ways.

I'd like to share an incident that happened a long time ago. Although it was a minor occurrence, it's the kind of thing that happens all the time. I was in college, at a football game with friends, and we'd been drinking.

The man in front of us was sitting between his two sons, one maybe ten, the other twelve. During the game, the man's shirt gradually pulled out from his pants and his backside was exposed.

When I noticed this, I turned to my friends, whispered, "Watch this," reached forward, and poured some beer down the back of his pants. I thought it was a very funny thing to do. The people with me thought it was funny too and we laughed among ourselves.

The man turned around and looked at me. His boys were watching him closely to see what he would do. Because we had been loud, I'm sure he knew that we were drunk and that if he confronted us we (I) might cause a scene or start a fight. So he did nothing.

He was obviously angry but felt powerless in the situation. I mumbled "Sorry about that," and pretended it was an accident. But that wasn't true. It was a joke to me and I did it to show off. And I did it because that is the kind of thing people do when they're drunk. The man got up with his sons and moved to a different part of the stadium. I never saw him again, but I still remember the incident. It was a mean thing for me to do. I humiliated the man in front of his kids. Then I dared him to do something about it.

How angry and embarrassed he must have felt! I wonder how

many times he thought about the incident before finally putting it out of his mind. I wonder what his sons thought. Were they mad at their dad for not standing up for himself as the victim of a thoughtless prank. Did it spoil their day together?

What I did was self-centered and selfish, done at another person's expense. I didn't care about that man's feelings.

That's not the kind of person I was brought up to be, and it's not the kind of person I am today. But it was the way I behaved when I was drunk.

I have sons now, and I take them to football games. And we sit near people who are drinking and insensitive. I have a lot of empathy for the man I humiliated fifteen years ago. I have a good sense of how he felt. I wish I knew who he was. After all this time, I'd like to apologize to him.

We hear about all the big problems caused by drinking. I wonder how many little problems like this one occur every day, all around us. Drunkenness can hurt people in so many ways.

Teach your kids that drunkenness is not funny—that it often hurts others. You can do it in two ways—by talking to them about drinking and, of course, by setting a good example.

Prevention principle: Let your children know at a very early age that you do not consider drunk jokes funny, that laughing at drunkenness—real or pretended—is inappropriate. They will be more inclined to grow up believing that drunkenness is not humorous, but hurtful, not only to the person who's drinking, but to others too.

15

Nothing to do but drink

Okay, now I'm really mad. The hair is standing up on the back of my neck.

There's a guy going around talking to high school kids about drinking and driving. There's nothing wrong with that, of course, but read on. He was quoted in a small town paper as saying, "...the adults of the world have done nothing for teenagers. We made playgrounds for the little kids, rated the movies 'R' and have bars for ourselves—we've left you with nothing to do."

"On a Friday or Saturday night in (the name of their town), what do you do?" he asked the students. "I know what you're doing— drinking—but if you're not doing that, what do you do?"

The students' response was unanimous: nothing.

What he's saying is that because we adults haven't given kids lots of things to do, there's nothing for them to do but drink. The kids love this, but I say it's a bunch of baloney. It's an excuse to drink. "Gee, if only we lived in Greenerville (or whatever the town may be that seems more interesting than their own) there'd be lots to do and we wouldn't have to drink." You know what the kids in Greenerville say about their own town? The same thing: there's nothing to do here but drink.

And so we (parents) feel guilty and scramble around trying to find things for our kids to do to keep them out of trouble and away from drugs and booze. But guess what? We'll never win. As long as we take the responsibility for keeping kids entertained, we're going to lose. The kids are going to say, "I'm bored" and "What's next?" and "It better be good or we're going to drink."

I hate that "what are you going to do for me next?" attitude, especially when it comes to trying to keep youngsters from drinking. It's not our job to entertain kids. Around our house when a child complains about being bored, we say, "Fine, go to bed." All of a sudden the kid finds a hundred things to do.

It's not my job or your job or the community's job to entertain young people. It's the kids' job–they can use their own brains and resources. If kids are looking seriously for ways to put meaning into their lives and enjoy themselves, then they will find support from all directions. But if they're looking to us to entertain them, in an attempt to keep them off the beer and the pot, forget it.

The next time the kids in your town say there's nothing to do but drink, you could tell them to:

- Go home: help your parents; study to improve your grades; wash the dishes; read a book; clean your room; hose down the car; get to know how your parents really feel; help your brothers and sisters; help your grandparents; cook a meal; mow the lawn; shovel the walk. Begin to show your appreciation for what others have done for you.

- Go to your church or temple: help the poor; visit the sick; cheer the lonely; pray for the needy; help the elderly; give your time to your priest or minister or rabbi. Learn the joy of giving rather than receiving.

- Go to your community: get a job; learn a skill; win a scholarship; volunteer your time; become a Big Brother (Sister) to a little kid; tutor handicapped children; clean up your town; help kids who may be in over their heads with alcohol and drugs. Get involved in your town and make it a better place to live.

I'm not saying that a community should not provide for its youth. I believe young people should have opportunities for growth and enjoyment. But those opportunities are already available in most communities if kids will only look for them. And if they are not there, certainly the town will respond to its youth and help them create some significant activities.

But what bugs me is the attitude that "it's your job to entertain me—and if you don't do it right, I'm going to drink." I refuse to feel guilty and be used as an excuse to drink.

58

Prevention principle: Parents who believe that keeping kids entertained and busy enough will prevent them from getting into drugs or alcohol—and who therefore cram their kids' lives with nonstop activities—are living according to a false premise. Kids not only can use this parental belief to manipulate parents into providing entertainment, but to blame parents if they *do* develop drug problems. Kids with the ingenuity and resources to keep themselves entertained are less likely to resort to the "highs" of alcohol and other drug use.

16

Contracts and controversy

A few days ago our daughter came home with a Students Against Driving Drunk (SADD) *Contract for Life*. A speaker had been at her high school to encourage students to use the contract and to stir up enough interest to begin a SADD group.

You may have heard of this *Contract for Life* or had your son or daughter bring one home. They've been getting a lot of publicity in our area, some good, some bad.

Under the terms of this contract, parents agree to provide transportation at any time and any place if the youth feels he or she has had too much to drink to drive safely, no questions asked (at least at the time). Parents also agree not to drink and drive. The contract is signed both by the young person and by the parents.

The back of the SADD contract in essence tells parents that, while we (parents) have tried to keep our kids off alcohol and drugs, whatever we're doing is not working very well, and we need to face the reality that our kids are likely to drink and use drugs. So we might as well do what we can to prevent them from getting killed in a car accident.

When I first heard about the contract, it seemed like a good idea. After all, who wants their kids driving after they've been drinking, risking injury or perhaps even death?

But there's another side—a controversial side—to the *Contract for Life*.

The contract's purpose is to prevent drinking and driving by kids. Because of the specific focus, many parents (and kids) feel that signing the contract is saying, or at least implying, that it's okay for kids to drink as long as they don't drive.

Some parents are concerned that the contract ignores all the other problems alcohol causes teenagers. In addition, because the

61

contract implies that teenage drinking is unavoidable, some parents may feel that their desire for their child to remain alcohol-free is not realistic, so they might as well give up and give in.

Several organizations, including the National PTA and the National Federation of Parents for Drug-Free Youth, have spoken out against the *Contract for Life*.

These organizations (and ours, the Alcoholism Council of Nebraska, Lincoln) believe that it is both desirable and possible to have alcohol- and drug-free kids.

My wife and I would not sign the contract with our teenagers. Instead we wrote our own contract based on the ideas of nationally syndicted columnist Sue Rusche. It goes like this:

- We expect you not to drink alcohol until you are of legal age. Because there is alcoholism in our family, we would like you to abstain even after you are of legal age. But if, at that time, you do drink, drink small amounts, do not become intoxicated, and never drive after drinking.

- If you ever find yourself in a situation in which you are with friends or people who have been drinking, call us and we will gladly come and get you.

- As parents, we will support you by setting a good example and not drinking. (Other parents may choose to vow that they will drink small amounts infrequently and never drink on evenings when their kids are out and may need a ride.)

Some families, parent networks, and high schools around the country have developed their own contracts for students and parents.

Assuming that teenagers inevitably will drink or implying that it's okay for them to drink as long as they don't drive isn't teaching them to be responsible. It's encouraging them to break the law. It's also putting them at risk for all the other problems that alcohol can cause young people.

I know that SADD's intentions are good. They have developed some worthwhile programs, including peer counseling, and have sponsored many alcohol- and drug-free events. It is unfortunate that their excellent work has been so clouded by the controversy surrounding the *Contract for Life*.

I believe that I can expect my kids to obey the law and remain alcohol- and drug-free. And I won't buckle under when I'm told, "Well, everybody's doing it [using alcohol and other drugs]." Everybody *isn't* doing it, and, even if they were, that still wouldn't make it right.

Some parents feel that letting their kids drink is treating them like adults. I think just the opposite. Expecting kids to obey the law and grow up alcohol- and drug-free is treating them like the mature responsible adults we hope they will soon become.

Prevention principle: Work out a contract in your family based on responsibilities of children as well as parents—and on the expectation that young people will not drink until they are of legal age and will not use illegal drugs. Do not assume that kids will drink no matter what and therefore address just part of the problem—drinking and driving, for instance.

17

Prevention begins at home

A good parent-child relationship—one that builds self-worth in children—is important in preventing alcohol and drug problems. The closer a young person is to her mom and dad, and the better a young person feels about himself, the less risk there is for alcohol and drug problems to develop.

This makes sense for a couple of reasons. First, the more a child feels cared for by parents, the happier and more well-adjusted the child is likely to be. There is less need for alcohol and drugs to fill a void. Second, the stronger the relationship between parent and child, and the higher the self-worth of the child, the less susceptible he or she will be to peer pressure—especially peer pressure to use alcohol and drugs.

Over the past few years I have worked extensively with parents. I always ask them, "What are some things you do to get closer to your children and to build their self-worth?" I would like to pass on to you some of their suggestions:

- *Use the three-minute special.* Set aside three minutes a day for you and your child. Make it a special time for just the two of you. Go to a private area in your home, away from distractions, and talk about anything your child wants to talk about. Do it every day, same time, same place. Pretty soon you will both be looking forward to your little retreat.

- *Catch a kid being good.* Be on the lookout for times when your child is doing something neat and let him know you like it. The average parent gives eight negatives to a child for every positive (quit twirling your hair, your room's a mess, your shirt's hanging out, etc.) Make the ratio of positive to negative more even.

- *Avoid "skin thirst."* All people, especially kids, need to be touched. Remember how a touch, a hug, or a friend's arm around you makes you feel warm, important, and accepted? Kids feel the same way. They love touching and need it. Touch your kid often.

- *Clarify your role.* Be tough but loving. Let your kids know that you are their parents, not their buddies. Being a parent means saying no at times, not protecting kids from every little hurt. Let them grow by experiencing life, a life that may include some pain.

- *Use the time or money plan.* Give kids a little extra of the one you don't have. If money is scarce in your family, scrape up an extra fifty cents or dollar once in a while and add it to your child's allowance. Your child will think, "Gee, Mom (or Dad) must really think I'm special. Money is tight in our home, but they're giving me a little extra this week." If you are very busy, set aside an extra half hour or hour now and then for your child. Your child will think, "Wow, Dad (or Mom) is really busy, I must be special to him (or her)."

- *Teach kids to care.* Teach them to care about you and others. Teach your kids empathy. Ask them questions like, "How do you think you would feel inside if you were the kid everyone in your class picked on?" Increase kids' self-worth by giving them responsibilities around the house, even when they are young. Encourage your kids to adopt an older couple in the neighborhood—shovel their walk, mow their lawn, and run errands for them. Kids can learn early in life that happiness comes more from serving others than from self-indulgence (especially indulgence in alcohol and drugs).

- *Talk about family values.* What does your family stand for? What's acceptable and not acceptable? Kids should be proud to be part of their family. Knowing what's right and what's wrong for your family gives kids an anchor and specific guidelines. This will help kids when peer pressure strikes. They'll already have a base from which to make decisions and to say no.

- *Laugh.* Have fun with your kids. Be a kid again yourself

sometimes. Keep your sense of humor. Life is meant to be enjoyed.

Kids with fewer alcohol and drug problems come from close families that help build their self-worth, from families who openly talk about alcohol and drugs, and from families whose parents have set limits and established consequences for alcohol and drug use. They have parents who set good examples by not using illegal drugs and by modeling low-risk choices—including abstinence—in the use of alcohol.

Almost all parents love their kids. Unfortunately, not all kids feel loved or feel good about themselves. Start helping them today.

Prevention principle: Build the kind of close family in which members respect and support each other's self-worth. Talk openly about alcohol and other drugs. Set limits and establish consequences for alcohol and drug use. Be examples for your children; don't use illegal drugs, and, when it comes to alcohol, be sure that you are modeling behaviors you would like them to follow.

18

Guidelines for adults who drink

I suppose that some people who will read these essays may come to the conclusion that I'm against all drinking—maybe even a prohibitionist. But that's not true. I'm not against drinking. I'm only against drinking that hurts people or puts them at risk for problems.

So rather than draw the line between drinking or not drinking, I draw the line between low-risk drinking and high-risk drinking. I believe adults should be free to drink as long as there's no danger and no one gets hurt. I also support people's right not to drink and believe it is in some people's best interest (underage kids, for example) not to drink at all.

This essay offers specific low-risk drinking guidelines for parents to use, and they're offered for three reasons. First, following them will greatly reduce the risk of any alcohol-related problem happening to you. Second, following these guidelines will allow you to set a good example for your kids. Third, the guidelines are given so that you can begin teaching them to your kids. That way, when your kids grow up, and if they choose to drink, they will have learned guidelines which may help them avoid problems.

By offering these suggestions to you we are not encouraging either you or your kids to drink. But if you do drink and follow these guidelines, you're likely to drink problem-free. And if your kids choose to drink when they become adults, they will have been taught guidelines to use which will greatly reduce their risk for problems. And remember—we recommend no use of illegal drugs ever—by adults or kids.

Here are the guidelines:

- Don't drink at all if you have a family history of alcoholism (it runs in families), you are alcoholic (either recovering or active), you are underage, you are pregnant, you are taking medication, or you are intending to drive.

- For adults with no family history of alcoholism, we recommend never exceeding a top limit of one-and-a-half ounces of absolute alcohol on any given day. This translates into three one-ounce shots of 100 proof liquor, three cans of beer, or three four-ounce glasses of table wine. We also recommend never exceeding a top limit of twelve drinks per week.

- One day's unused ration can't be saved up and used later. In other words, you can't abstain all week and then have twelve drinks on Saturday night.

- Drinks should be consumed at a rate of no more than one per hour. At this rate the average person can metabolize the alcohol in the first drink before the second drink is consumed.

- Before drinking, consider the situation you are in. For example, driving a car, operating machinery, and swimming, to name a few, are situations that should be alcohol-free.

- Before drinking, consider your own "state of being." If you are tired, you have been sick, or you haven't eaten, maybe your best decision is to abstain and reconsider tomorrow.

- Finally, if you use alcohol as a problem-solver, your problems will multiply. Using alcohol (or other drugs) to cope with stress, loneliness, depression, or any other "human experience" does not permit the development of other, healthier ways of coping.

As you can see, a good deal of thought needs to go into any decision to drink. About seven of ten kids will drink when they become adults. They have much to learn if they are to make consistent decisions about drinking and drugs that will not result in harm to themselves or others.

This information needs to be fed to our kids as they are growing up, at times when they are receptive to learning. We can feed information to our kids two ways: first, by talking to them; and, second, by demonstrating low-risk drinking or not drinking at all.

If you talk a good game but drink in a high-risk way, don't be surprised if your kids have problems.

Note: These guidelines are general suggestions that I believe may help many people who choose to drink. They are not intended as ironclad rules. Clearly each person needs to assess his or her own ability to drink. If you have any concern about your physical condition, consult with your doctor about the impact alcohol may have on you.

Prevention principle: If you do not choose abstinence (because you are alcoholic or from an alcoholic family or for any other reason), model low-risk drinking for your children. If you drink, drink according to the guidelines given here—and, of course, don't use illegal drugs.

19

'Taking off' and 'hanging out'

There's an old saying that members of Alcoholics Anonymous have used for years. It goes like this: "If you hang around a barber shop long enough, you're going to get a haircut."

What this means is that if a recovering alcoholic spends a lot of time in bars or with people who are drinking, it's only a matter of time before he or she starts drinking again. In other words, if you want to stay sober, stay away from drinking situations.

Now the same idea applies to kids and alcohol and drugs. Young people who hang around with kids who drink and use drugs are also going to drink and use drugs. In fact the biggest single predictor of alcohol/drug abuse is having friends who use. If your kids are hanging out with friends who drink and use, it's only a matter of time before your own kids will be involved. This makes sense. After all, how many times can a kid say no to peers before finally saying, "Aw, what the heck."

We've had some real battles around our house when it comes to our kids' friends. There have been times when we have felt it necessary to step in and stop our kids from spending time with other kids we felt were not good influences, and who had parents that would not support us. As you know, a kid doesn't give up a friend (bad influence or not) without a fight. But being a parent often means being unpopular with kids–and saying no to them.

Here are a few suggestions that might help:

- Set reasonable curfews for your kids and be clear about the people and places that are off limits to them.

- Get to know your child's friends and their parents. It is difficult to pick up the phone and call another parent, but the other parent almost always appreciates it. As parents, begin to support each other.

- Know who your kids will be with, where they will be, what they will be doing, and when they will be home. Spend a few minutes with your kids when they get home to make sure everything went all right.

- Don't allow kids to just "take off" to "hang out." The more unsupervised nights outside the home, the greater the chance of alcohol/drug problems.

- Make sure your kids know your rules about alcohol and drug use. Set consequences ahead of time and enforce them if the rules are broken.

Influencing kids in their choice of friends when we can is one of the tough jobs we face as parents. Any influence we have needs to come from a base of knowledge about those young friends, their activities and behavior, and their families. Kids don't often buy judgments of their peers based on our instincts. They may not, in fact, buy our judgments at all. We may be very unpopular with them on the subject of their friends. But try to remember that it's not our goal to be popular with our kids. If we try to be our kids' best buddies, they've lost their parents.

It's our goal to raise children as best we can. And that means seeing that they are in a safe environment outside the home as well as inside the home. Remember—helping your kids think through their choices of friends is not meddling; it's caring. And the sooner we start, the easier it will be as they grow older. Someday they'll thank us.

Prevention principle: Know where your kids are and who their friends are. When their friends obviously are alcohol/drug users—or seem to be influencing peers to use alcohol or other drugs—don't be afraid to make those associations off limits for your children.

20

You are what you wear

The other day, as I was walking through the lobby of the building in which I work, I noticed a boy waiting for the elevator. He seemed to be about thirteen or fourteen years old, maybe in seventh or eighth grade. What caught my attention were the clothes the boy had on. He wore a T-shirt with a drug slogan on it and a hat with a beer logo across the front.

The first thing that went through my mind was, "This kid is going to be a drinker and a drug-user. He may not be using now, but he will be soon."

Why did I think that? Well, partly it was just common sense. By wearing "drug and alcohol" clothes, this kid is telling the world that alcohol and drugs are important to him. He thinks about them a lot and he's proud of it. And he wants people to know about his commitment to them.

My guess is also backed up by research. One of the strongest predictors of future alcohol or drug problems is holding favorable attitudes about alcohol and drugs before beginning to use. In other words, the beginning of use (and trouble) is preceded by values favorable to use. As I said, it's only a matter of time for this kid.

Attitudes about alcohol and other drugs develop slowly over a period of time. Because of this, parents can have a great influence on whether or not kids develop healthy or unhealthy attitudes about alcohol and drugs.

One way we influence our kids is, of course, by our own behavior. The way we drink or use drugs is a quiet but powerful message that says, "This is the way for you to do it."

A second influence on kids is the type of rules we set for them. In our home, we have very clear rules: kids in our home do not use alcohol or drugs. Our family does not allow clothes with alcohol or drug messages on them, nor do we allow a style of dress associated with the drug culture. We do not allow music, posters, or activities (such as movies and concerts) that portray alcohol or drugs as acceptable, normal, or beneficial for young people.

Here are some suggestions on how to help kids develop healthy attitudes about alcohol and drugs:

- Start talking to kids early and often. Let them know that drug use or underage alcohol use is unacceptable. Teach them that getting drunk or high is not a part of growing up, that they don't have to drink or use drugs to be happy or fit in, and that being drunk or high is not funny, but dangerous.

- Don't let your kids have or wear clothes that have alcohol or drug messages on them. Don't let kids have beer signs or drug-oriented posters in their rooms.

- Monitor your kids' activities; make music, movies, and concerts that glorify alcohol and drugs off limits to kids.

- Try to keep your kids away from peers who use alcohol and/or drugs or who have attitudes favorable to use. Trust your judgment in this area.

Remember, kids don't grow up alcohol- and drug-free by luck. It takes thought and effort. The sooner you begin, the better the odds for success.

Prevention principle: Try to prevent attitudes favorable to alcohol and other drug use in your children (a predictor of later drinking or using): ban clothing and posters with pro-drinking or pro-drug messages; keep kids away from activities or associates that give them these messages; let them know clearly that—in your rule book—drug use or underage alcohol use is unacceptable.

21

'Wasted'—and a life wasted

My friend was the first on the scene. "It was about 5 A.M. and I was in bed asleep," she said. "I heard a car drive up the street very fast and I thought I heard kids laughing." She heard the terrible crash in front of her house and, after a few seconds of silence, a voice yelling for help. She called 911 and ran down to the street.

"I'll never forget the girl lying in the street on the cold concrete," she said. "There was no blood and there were no scratches. She looked so pretty. She appeared tall and slender. She seemed to be asleep. But somehow I knew she was dying."

And she was. She was dying from massive head and chest injuries caused from being thrown from a Jeep when it crashed into a parked car and flipped over. She would live for three days on a life-support system. But she never really had a chance. She was seventeen years old.

The young man who had been driving was going to live. He had been drinking. He, too, was thrown out of the Jeep upon impact. His face was banged up, his nose broken, but he was not severely injured. "He seemed to be in shock," my friend said. "He kept crying out, 'Help me, help me—'"

"It was five in the morning—one car, two kids. I knew right away it was alcohol. God, what a waste...," she said. "I've seen people die before, but this was the worst. Because of the alcohol. Two kids just trying to have fun. I saw some beer cans lying in the street. I don't know if they flew out of the Jeep or if someone else had thrown them there earlier. I hated those beer cans. I was so angry at what alcohol had just done to the two people lying in the street. Especially the girl. One minute she's laughing and the next minute she's dying."

The accident happened quite a while ago, but it still affects my friend. "Every time I pull up in front of the house, I see her lying there. When I'm in bed at night I still hear his voice calling out for help. I feel sorry for the girl," she said, "but at least it's over for her. It will never be over for him. He's got to live with that night for the rest of his life."

The girl is dead. The boy went to jail. Suits have been filed. And the parents will be grieving forever. The events can't be changed.

I'm bothered that they call what happened an "accident." That's a misleading term. It sounds as though that sad event was a chance happening—a quirk of fate, a stroke of bad luck. That's not true. This fatal collision happened because the driver had a blood alcohol content of .145, far above the legal limit. So what happened was no accident; it was a death caused by drinking. Let's call it what it was.

Young people must understand that anyone in this kind of situation is at great risk for tragedy. Most kids don't believe it. "It could never happen to me—I'm immune." "I'm too smart (or too strong or too lucky or too young)." We can start by teaching our children that anyone can get hurt or killed if they drink too much. Anyone. Kids (and many adults) think that they can somehow pull it all together in an emergency, sober up in an instant. But that's not what happens when we consume alcohol. We just can't control ourselves the way we think we can.

I wonder how many parents say to themselves, "Well, my kid might drink a little, but at least he's not on drugs." Probably a lot. But drinking is not an alternative to drugs. Alcohol *is* a drug and every bit as dangerous as other drugs. In fact, alcohol-related accidents are the leading cause of death among our young men and women.

A postscript: The young man has received some counseling for his drinking problem. That's the one glimmer of light in this dark tale. I hope he does well.

Prevention principle: Start early to teach your kids that anyone of any age can get hurt—or even killed—when drinking too much. Avoid the all-too-typical attitude: "At least they're not taking drugs; they're only drinking." Remember: alcohol *is* a drug!

22

The cutting edge

My friend Charlie and I sometimes talk about preventing alcohol and drug problems among kids. We meet at the local YMCA. During the lunch hour he swims and I run. We meet afterward in the locker room and talk.

As Charlie sees it, the problem is that the "cutting edge" is getting further and further out. What he means is that the limits of acceptable behavior for young people continue to be stretched. The behavior of the wildest kids, the cutting edge some years ago, now seems tame when compared to many of the things young people are doing today.

Charlie gives an example of what he means. He grew up in a small town in the late '50s. Charlie was on the high school basketball team, a "straight arrow" group. One day when he and some teammates were sitting in the local coffee shop, another teammate wearing a letter jacket walked in with a cigarette hanging out of his mouth. The accepted behavior for high school athletes in that little town at the time did not include smoking. So Charlie and his buddies escorted their smoking teammate into an alley out back and "convinced" him to give up the habit.

Things have really changed for young people since those days. They've changed not only when it comes to smoking, drinking, and drug-using, but also in the areas of sexual activity, attitudes toward authority, and school behavior, to name a few. What only the wildest kids did when we were young is now considered "normal." In fact, some kids today are doing things we didn't even know *could* be done.

What's the problem with the change in the cutting edge? It's not that we don't want our kids to have fun or to be happy. We do. It's just that we don't want them to get hurt, and that's the problem with the cutting edge. Too many kids are getting involved in behavior that hurts them.

Why has the cutting edge moved so far to such a dangerous point? There are many reasons. I suspect that some of the reasons include the breakdown of traditional family values, a rapidly changing world, more money and time available to kids, and a barrage of pro-alcohol and pro-drug messages in advertisements, movies, and music. All of these things combine to allow or even encourage dangerous "at the edge" behavior by young people.

So how do we protect our kids in a world that's becoming a more dangerous place for them to live?

We do it by pulling back the cutting edge. And we do it in our own family—with our own kids. We do it by being tough but loving parents. We have the courage to say, "Just because everyone is doing it does't mean you're going to do it." We have the courage and commitment to say no to certain friends, films, concerts, and styles of clothing. We set limits through curfews and establish what people and what places are off limits for our kids. We set expectations of no alcohol or drug use by our kids and set serious consequences for our kids if they do not honor our expectations. We present good models for our kids by practicing what we preach in all areas, and, when it comes to alcohol and drugs, we never use illegal drugs and we never drink to the point of intoxication.

Raising kids is tougher now than it was back in Charlie's high school days. The cutting edge has moved a lot. But we can pull that edge back a little, if we start at home.

Prevention principle: Pull back the "cutting edge," or the outer limits of acceptable behavior for youth (and adults), especially in the area of alcohol and other drug use. Do this by setting standards in your own home, by not giving in to young people's "everybody does it" arguments—and by living up to the kind of standards that make you a healthy example for your kids.

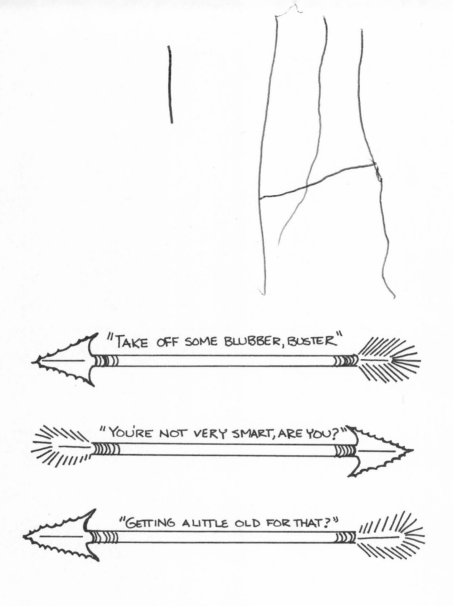

23

Nice head, Number 32

Recently I went to a university basketball game. I was looking forward to this game because the opponents had a fine basketball tradition and I knew they would be coming to town with some great athletes.

Our seats were supposed to be high in the rafters, but, because many of the students had left town that week for vacation, the ushers opened up the floor-level bleachers to anyone. My stepson, Mike, and I rushed down and found two wonderful seats, right below the best reserved seats in the house and so close to the court we could hear every sound the players made. What luck!

It was an exciting, seesaw battle, and we were loving it until an incident occurred in the second half.

The head of the opponents' best athlete, Number 32, was somewhat misshapen. It appeared to have a ridge on top, the kind of malformation that might have been caused by the use of forceps at birth.

Number 32 had just been fouled near us and was standing at the free-throw line getting ready to shoot when a guy in the reserved seats just behind me suddenly yelled out, "Nice head, Thirty-two." And then he yelled it again, "Hey, Thirty-two—nice head!" Everyone near us could hear him.

Mike and I looked at each other. Our eyes said, "What an awful, cruel thing to say." I turned around to see who had yelled and saw that he was a well-dressed man, probably in his early thirties. Sitting with him were his four little children (one on his lap) and a woman I assume was his wife. The kids all seemed to be grade-school age.

I thought, What a terrible thing to say to another person and what a terrible example to set in front of those little kids. And sure enough, a few minutes later one of his kids recognized a local TV announcer at courtside and began screaming out his name again and again totally unaware that he was embarrassing the man and annoying people around him who were trying to watch the game. And the father, of course, said nothing to his son.

I felt really bad for Number 32. So did Mike and probably a lot of the other people who heard what this guy said. I don't know if Number 32 heard the remarks or not. Probably so, but maybe he can tune stuff like that out now. He's probably heard it before, maybe so many times that he's numb to the pain.

I write about this incident for two reasons.

First, I wonder how many people who may be a little different have been driven to alcohol or drugs as a way to deaden the pain that has been inflicted on them by the cruelty of other people. Sure, I know there are lots of reasons why people get into problems with drugs and alcohol, but if you're around enough people like the guy sitting behind me, the booze and drugs can begin to look like a good way out.

Second, I'm reminded again about the influence that parents have over their kids. Unless some sort of intervention takes place, those four little kids are likely to grow up and hurt people just like their dad does.

Isn't it time we start caring about each other a little more?

Prevention principle: Train children to be sensitive about the hurts of others—and hope that others will be sensitive to *their* hurts and differences. Too often, hurting people seek to deaden pain through drugs and alcohol.

24

A talk with Billy Martin

"Little kids look up to us. We've got to provide proper role models"—Billy Martin.

Hi, Billy. I read what you had to say about drugs in *The Sporting News* a while back. Thought it was great. I couldn't agree with you more. Like you say, we've got to go after those drug-users in baseball real hard. We've got to get those crack-eaters, cocaine-snorters, potheads, and speed freaks out of the game.

You say that if we catch players using drugs we ought to make them forfeit their salaries and their pensions as well. A little stiff, maybe, but you're on the right track, Billy. After all, kids look up to these guys and we can't be giving them bad examples to follow. Hats off to you, Billy—not everyone has the guts to make such a public statement.

But there's one little area that I don't quite understand, Billy. I happened to read about your involvement in a barroom brawl. Drinking seems to be a big part of your life. In fact it seems to me as if drinking somehow is connected to most of those fights you get into and those jobs you lose.

So there seems to be a slight contradiction here. You want us to nail people who use certain drugs, but it's fine for you to drink the way you do. Do you know that alcohol is a drug, Billy? It just happens to come in a liquid form instead of a powder. You want us to kick a marijuana smoker out of the game but turn our heads to a barroom fight with players on your own team. You even make money off the drug alcohol, Billy. You know, "Tastes great—less filling."

But you think we should get rid of the druggies and be good role models for the kids.

You know what Billy? I think you're a hypocrite. At the very least, you should keep quiet about drugs and role-modeling. I believe that if you ever really want to help kids, you can start by examining your own drinking behavior, changing it, and beginning to make amends to all the people your drinking may have hurt.

It's a confusing world for kids to grow up in, Billy. They need all the help we can give them. The last person they need to listen to is a guy who seems, in my opinion, to have a drinking problem telling them about drugs.

What do you think about all this, Billy? Billy? Billy . . . ?

Prevention principle: All the anti-drug preaching in the world falls flat when those who preach it are questionable role models—such as people who seem, judging by media reports, to have a drinking problem. Try to point out such hypocrisies to your kids, so they can understand that alcohol is indeed a drug.

25

Rock and the 'right to party'

Erin came to me filled with hope and excitement. She wanted to ask something, and had chosen me to talk to rather than her mom because I'm a softer touch. She's a smart kid.

"The Beastie Boys are coming to town next week for a concert," she said. "I just got invited to go with my friend and her dad. Can I go? Can I? Can I?"

It didn't take long for me to decide what my answer to her would be. After all, for some time now I've been talking to parents about the need to monitor pro-alcohol and pro-drug concerts and movies and to keep kids away from them. I had also heard a little bit about the Beastie Boys and thought they might not be a good influence. So I said what any strong parent would say, particularly one who wants his kids to like him and has a hard time saying no.

"Go ask your mom," I said.

The smile disappeared from her face. That was the last thing she wanted to hear. With her hope fading fast, she trudged off to ask her mom, fully expecting to hear the worst.

"The Beastie Boys are coming to town, Mom," she said. "I've been invited to go, can I go?"

"The Beastie Boys," my wife said. "Ah yes, I've heard of them. Don't they have a big song out? What's the name of that song anyway?"

"'Fight for Your Right...to Party,'" Erin mumbled.

"Yes, that's the one," replied my wife. "What I'd like you to do," she continued, shifting the responsibility (and burden of proof) back to Erin, "is to get a pencil and paper and write down all the reasons why going to the Beastie Boys concert will make you a better person. Then, find the words to some of their songs and write them down. Finally, ask your older brothers and sisters what they've heard about the Beastie Boys and ask them if they think the Beastie Boys will be a good influence on you. When you've done all that, we'll sit down, look it all over and make a decision."

After some deep thought, a little research, and a bit of conversation with her older siblings, Erin sadly but wisely decided she didn't want to go to the concert anyway, and returned her pencil and blank sheet of paper to their drawer. The matter was settled. She had given up her "fight to her right to party."

A week later the concert was held, and a review appeared in the following morning's paper. The decision not to allow Erin to go to the concert had been the right one. According to the review, when they weren't singing, the Boys' topics of discussion were women, beer, and sex. Their jokes were obscene. A giant phallic symbol was set on the stage and a crew member trotted around the stage with a big beer sign. A go-go girl undulated in a huge birdcage for the entire concert. Her costume was so skimpy that it probably violated local obscenity laws. The concert ended with a rousing version of their hit song, "Fight for Your Right." A fitting ending to a concert which, in my opinion, gave a clear message to the young audience: sex and alcohol—it's perfectly fine to get involved in both. Live it up kids. Get loaded. Have sex. Have fun. No problem. Most of the kids present were young teens or younger.

After the concert, a fourteen-year-old intoxicated girl was sexually assaulted. The Boys and their crew, a few thousand dollars richer, packed up and went on, probably not giving a damn about the mess they were leaving behind and the kids that were going to get hurt by their sex and alcohol messages.

We would have made a big mistake if we'd allowed Erin to go to this concert. The parents of 3,325 kids in our town made a big mistake. This was not harmless fun. It was inviting kids to play with fire. No wonder kids get all messed up when they are exposed to junk like that!

The message we give to our kids is clear. No drinking, no drugs, no sex. We have these expectations for one simple reason: we love our kids and don't want them to get hurt.

I didn't do a very good job in saying no to Erin. Saying no to kids is hard for me. I was also concerned about what the parents of the friend who had invited Erin would think of me. But the bottom line was that she didn't go, and it was the correct decision. I urge you to say no to your kids in similar situations.

Prevention principle: Say no to kids' pleas to go to concerts, movies, and other events where sex-and-alcohol messages are blatant. (If you don't know what the messages will be, find out—ahead of time.) Saying no isn't easy but it *is* the right thing to do.

26

A gutsy parent

In my part of the country—and very likely yours—one of the big problems is parents' buying alcohol for kids.

I'd like to tell you a story about a time this happened, and a friend of mine who had the guts to do something about it.

His name is Gene. He's a coach and lives in a small town near here.

One Friday night Gene's thirteen-year-old stepdaughter asked and received permission to go to a friend's house to spend the night at a slumber party. She had even shown her parents an invitation. But it was a phony invitation; she never went to a slumber party.

Instead, she went to a beer party. An acquaintance of hers was celebrating her sixteenth birthday. A birthday present from her dad, a well-known farmer in the area, was a beer party for the girl and her friends. More than one hundred kids showed up. Car keys were collected from the young drivers at the door and returned at the end of the evening at the discretion of the birthday girl! Some adults were present, but they stayed in a part of the house that was away from the kids and their alcohol. Several young people, boys and girls, spent the night at the house. Gene's stepdaughter got drunk and spent the night.

The next day Gene found out what had happened. He was very angry and called the birthday girl's dad.

"He defended what he had done. He didn't think he had done anything wrong," Gene told me. "Finally, the man said, 'What do you want from me?' He had me. I didn't know what I wanted. So I just hung up."

The next day, while I was reading the newspaper, I happened to glance at an advice column. The words leaped out at me. A parent who had gone through a similar experience was asking the columnist for advice. The advice was simple: there was only one way to deal with parents who provide beer parties for kids—press charges.

And that's what Gene did, with the encouragement and support of his wife.

He had his daughter give a statement to the police. He found another angry parent whose daughter had also gone to the party. The second girl also gave a statement to the police.

As good fortune would have it, a supportive county attorney was willing to file two charges for procuring alcohol for a minor against the host. Soon thereafter the man pleaded guilty in front of a supportive judge and was sentenced to forty days in jail!

The message the judge gave was clear: if you buy alcohol for kids around here and get caught, you're in a bunch of trouble. In commenting on the case, the judge said, "The court finds that there is a very substantial problem in this country involving parties for minors with alcohol being served. The community must know that it is not only against the law, but they are endangering both the lives of their children during and immediately after these parties and also the future of their children, and making it commonplace, so that these children think nothing of consuming alcoholic beverages in large quantities. This court must send a message to the community that such actions cannot be condoned."

As you can imagine, this raised quite a fuss in the community. The newspaper was swamped with letters voicing people's opinions on what happened. Letters supporting Gene and the judge outnumbered those against their actions about eight to one. The story was picked up by other newspapers and publicized throughout the state.

"The people in the community were very supportive," said Gene. "I'd say at least seventy-five percent were on my side. But you know," he said, "I was so damn mad at what happened, I didn't care what anybody else thought."

That's not to say that it was a totally positive experience, particularly for Gene's kids. "My two teenage daughters took a lot of flack. It was tough on them. For a while they weren't included in their friends' activities. They don't regret what I did, but they wouldn't want me to do it again."

Would he do it again if faced with a similar situation? "In a minute," said Gene. "My kids wouldn't be too happy, but in the long run, they'd understand." And respect him too, I'll bet.

"It's had an effect," Gene said. The message is now out that parents who do this sort of thing will be punished if caught. In fact, soon after the first incident, a second parent was caught supplying alcohol to kids and she was sentenced to forty-five days in jail.

The birthday girl's father is still very upset and resentful, and that's too bad. But the number of open beer parties has gone down considerably, and far fewer area parents are buying alcohol for kids. In fact, one of the local all-night cafe owners said his late-night breakfast business has fallen off noticeably; there just are not as many kids out beer-partying and getting hungry afterwards.

Obviously what Gene did is not going to solve the alcohol and drug problems in his community, but it's a good start! And it's a wonderful example of what one parent can do, if he has the courage to stand up for his convictions. But Gene didn't do it alone. He had supportive law enforcement officers, a strong county attorney, and a judge who refused to look the other way. He also had friends and other community members who were willing to show their support by calling, by writing, or in some other way voicing their agreement.

All of these elements must fall into place for this kind of parental courage to work and to address this serious problem. If one "support" had caved in, perhaps nothing would have come of his pressing charges, and Gene would have been left out on a limb.

Gene thinks what he did is "no big deal." Maybe so, but I hope that if I find myself in a similar spot, I'll have the courage to do what Gene did.

Prevention principle: Have the courage to press charges against any parent who serves alcohol to minors. Your courage—plus community support—can cut down on the number of such potentially dangerous situations.

27

Mixed messages

I was in a classroom the other day talking to kids about alcohol and other drugs. It was a sixth-grade class, so the kids were about eleven or twelve years old.

I was really surprised at some of the things they said. First of all, most of the kids told me that they had drunk alcohol in a place other than their own homes, without parental supervision. In other words, most of them admitted to having drinking experiences with their friends. This concerned me because research in this area says that kids who get into alcohol at early ages, especially before age fifteen, are at high risk for developing alcohol and drug problems.

I was also concerned about the kids' attitude about alcohol. When I asked the question about how many had drunk alcohol outside of their own homes, some of them didn't raise their hands at first. But when they saw so many of their classmates putting their hands up, they raised theirs too. Apparently the pro-alcohol attitude in this sixth-grade classroom was so strong that the kids who hadn't drunk with friends were afraid to say so!

As we talked, it became obvious that most of the kids thought that getting drunk was cool—a grown-up thing to do—and that it had an important place in their future.

But what about using other drugs like marijuana or cocaine? The answer was unanimous. Absolutely not. According to these kids, none had tried them, none were ever going to, and anyone who did was stupid and an awful person.

Why such contrasting attitudes and behaviors when it comes to alcohol use and other drug use? How can kids so young be so "against" illegal drugs and so "for" alcohol? After all, alcohol *is* a drug, the drug that hurts far more young (and old) people than all other drugs combined.

This attitude that drugs are terrible but that alcohol is fine for everyone, including kids, does not happen by accident.

Let me give you a couple of examples that have caught my attention, examples that demonstrate how kids end up with this mixed-up and dangerous attitude.

Bruce Willis is a well-known TV and movie actor, the star of a very popular TV show, "Moonlighting." Willis also has appeared in an anti-drug public service announcement campaign on TV. His message was simple: stay away from drugs. Yet while he was telling people (including kids) to stay away from drugs, at the same time he was appearing in alcohol commercials. He was doing ads for wine coolers. So on one channel his message was to stay away from drugs, while on another channel his message was to drink alcohol. This is particularly frustrating to me because, at least in my area, wine-based drinks (wine coolers) are rapidly becoming the drug of choice among young kids.

Sports, both college and professional, are taking a hard line against the use of certain drugs by athletes. Most sports are pushing for—or are already requiring—drug testing for athletes. The public is also very much against the use of marijuana and cocaine by athletes, and the commissioner of professional baseball has said that baseball will soon be almost drug-free.

Oh, yeah? Well, what about alcohol use by athletes? Professional baseball players go right from the field into locker rooms that serve beer, lots of it. How many other jobs do you know of that, after each day's work, offer you all the beer you can drink, provided by your employer?

An article in *Sports Illustrated* a while back included a photo of a well-known baseball player, Fernando Valenzuela, being interviewed in the team's locker room. Appearing behind him in the photo were the players' lockers. Next to each player's name, at the top of the locker, was a "Lite" beer logo! That's right: beer logos on players' lockers in the dressing room.

When the New York Mets won the World Series, the players didn't wait until they got into the locker room to start drinking. The drinking began right on the pitcher's mound, with the players chugging champagne on national television. The "good times" then continued in the locker room and at an all-night party. A newsletter reported that the restaurant in which the party was held was nearly destroyed.

No wonder those little kids in the classroom had such confused attitudes about alcohol and other drugs: "Marijuana and cocaine are terrible, but getting bombed on alcohol is acceptable." After all, their heroes tell them that drugs are bad, but show them that alcohol is just fine.

Now, don't get me wrong. I'm very much against the use of drugs such as marijuana and cocaine. But I'm also against the implicit message given to kids that alcohol is harmless and not a drug.

Research seems to indicate that young people who get mixed messages about alcohol and drugs are more likely to have problems with them. This makes sense. If youngsters grow up believing that smoking pot is bad but getting drunk is okay, you've got kids who are probably going to get drunk and thus place themselves in high-risk situations.

While it may be a long time before our children stop receiving mixed messages from outside influences, we can at least provide consistent messages within our families. The message to our children should be simple:

Alcohol is a drug. It hurts more people than all other drugs combined. Alcohol differs from other drugs in that its use is legal in certain circumstances for some people (people of legal drinking age, for example). Low-risk drinking—drinking small amounts and avoiding intoxication–is acceptable behavior for most people and seems to be relatively risk-free. But this is a behavior reserved for adults. Besides, intoxication from alcohol is dangerous. Intoxicated people may hurt themselves and others.

Talk with your kids and see if they have picked up this pro-alcohol attitude. If they have, give them the correct information, and, when you see instances of mixed messages, point them out and discuss them with your children.

Prevention principle: Be on the alert for the subtle and not so subtle mixed messages that tell us—and our kids—that drinking alcohol is always acceptable, while other drugs are not. And set your kids straight. Alcohol, along with marijuana and cocaine and others, is a mood-altering chemical. It *is* a drug.

28

Seven reasons to say no

All the parents I've talked to want their kids to stay away from illegal drugs. However, a lot of parents struggle with whether or not they should allow their teenage children to drink. Some parents seem to think that, since so many young people drink, they should allow their children to go along with the crowd. But a lot of kids don't drink. And for good reasons. Here are seven reasons I've come up with:

- In the case of underage kids, it's against the law.

- Kids get hurt. Alcohol-related accidents are the leading cause of death and injury among teenagers.

- The earlier a person first uses alcohol, the greater the likelihood of progression to heavy use, and the less chance of stopping.

- Alcohol is a "gateway" drug for many young people. Most teens who use illegal drugs first used alcohol. The typical sequence is beer or wine, followed by cigarettes or hard liquor, then marijuana and other illegal drugs.

- A young person whose social life revolves around drinking enters adulthood handicapped, less able to find other sources of fun and relaxation. A social life built around alcohol robs young people of growth and contributes nothing to them personally, or to their family or community. An alcohol-centered existence is a selfish way of life, a waste.

- Alcohol problems for kids rarely occur in isolation. A kid into alcohol is at risk for a variety of problems: skirmishes with the law, problems at school, involvement with other drugs, cigarette-smoking, difficulties with relationships, increased sexual activity and unplanned pregnancy—to name a few.

● Finally, alcohol is just too seductive for kids. It can be a powerful escape from the tough issues a kid must face and work through. If kids drink to overcome shyness, to gain courage, to be comfortable with members of the opposite sex, to deal with fear, to avoid responsibilities and pain, then they are not learning important skills necessary to become competent adults. What a shame to allow our children to enter adulthood with a half-empty toolbox of coping skills.

I've listed seven reasons why teenagers should not drink. Can you think of as many reasons why they should?

Not all kids get physically or emotionally hurt by drinking. I know that. But I also know that every kid who starts drinking is at increased risk for a range of problems—some of which are very big. Is it worth the risk? I don't think so.

Prevention principle: Consider carefully these seven good reasons not to allow teenage children to drink alcohol—and add more of your own. Pass these reasons on to your kids when they give you the "everybody does it" argument about drinking.

29

Helping kids hurt themselves

If I could give a gift to every parent, it would be the ability to stop enabling. By enabling, I mean parents' protecting their children from experiencing the natural consequences of their own actions.

Enabling fosters unhealthy and destructive behavior in children and prevents them from becoming mature independent adults. By shielding kids from the natural consequences of their own actions, we do not allow them to see themselves as others see them. When we do this, we deprive them of opportunities to change, to feel good about themselves, and to be liked by others. Finally, parental enabling keeps kids from learning responsibility and how to care for others.

My son used to play with a child in our neighborhood. The child was pampered and spoiled and protected by his parents. He was a kid who got everything he wanted, and always had to have his way. Finally, my son decided he didn't want to play with him anymore.

Do you know what the boy's parents did? They got mad at *my* son for not playing with *their* son. They could not, or would not, see that the reason their child couldn't keep friends was his selfish, demanding behavior. That's what I mean by parental enabling. The boy's parents enabled his behavior to continue. And because of his behavior, his peers rejected him and will continue to reject him. As a result, his self-worth will be lousy.

This child's parents are not helping him; they are hurting him. If they really wanted to help him, they would say, "Of course, your friend doesn't want to play with you. Because of the way you act, no one would want to play with you. You're the one who has to change—not your friend. You need to learn how to be a good friend, and we will help you learn. For starters, being a good friend

117

means not always getting your way. It means learning to share with others and caring about other people's feelings."

If he learns to be a good friend, this child can feel good about himself and end up with friends. But if his parents continue to protect him and blame others for his problem, chances are he will never mature emotionally and never behave in ways that will result in high self-worth. His behavior will continue to cause others to reject him.

I've read stories about high school athletes who have been kicked off their teams for drinking. They knew the rules, but broke them anyway and got caught. The young athletes and their parents, instead of accepting the consequences of the behavior, took the issue to court, or pressured the school board or principal and forced the coaches to allow them to play.

This is enabling in its most harmful form. The parents protected the kids from the consequences of their drinking behavior, and deprived them of opportunities for growth. The parents taught them that rules were meant for others, not for them. They taught them that competing for their own personal glory was more important than obeying rules meant to help everyone. They taught their children to be self-centered: take care of yourself first; don't respect your coach, your school, or your team; go ahead and break the rules; drink—just don't get caught.

Perhaps these parents acted out of misguided love. Perhaps they thought they were helping their kids. Or maybe they were not so noble; maybe personal pride prompted them to protect their kids—and themselves. Regardless of the reason, their actions hurt their children, the coaches, and the others on the teams.

A loving response from the parents of these young athletes would have been: "The rules were made for everyone's welfare, including yours. You were wrong in drinking. You broke the rules, and you must pay the consequences. In spite of what you may believe now, this will make you a better person." Instead of raising Cain to enable their kids to repeat the behavior, they should have gone to the coaches and said something like: "Thanks, Coach, for caring enough about our child to enforce the rules, knowing your team would lose a player. We support you."

My wife is determined not to enable the kids in our family. She asks people to tell her when the kids are out of line or acting insensitive or uncaring about others. Instead of avoiding unpleasant news, she seeks the information. She keeps no secrets and protects no kids from their bad behavior. She shares with her friends the inappropriate as well as the good things they do. The kids cringe when she tells the bad stuff; they plead with her not to do it. "Sorry," she says. "If you don't like it when I tell people how you act, then you'll need to change your behavior. It's your problem, not mine."

It is difficult to recognize our enabling and still more difficult to stop doing it. But we need to stop enabling if we're going to help develop strong, caring, responsible children who like themselves.

If your child hurts others, yet you defend and protect him or her, you're hurting your child.

If your child gets into trouble with the law and you hire a fancy lawyer to find a loophole, you're hurting your child.

If your child gets caught drinking or using drugs at school and you're not supportive of the school's policy of consequences, you're hurting your child.

Kids who are enabled to continue behaviors that are inappropriate or harmful learn to blame others for their problems. They also learn to shift the responsibility for their own happiness to other people. If alcohol and drugs are added, the problems are multiplied, and your child can easily become a self-absorbed, blaming, emotionally dependent person with few skills to deal with reality.

Letting kids experience the consequences of their behavior means that we must let them hurt at times. But these are temporary hurts, nothing like the lifelong pain that can result from parental enabling.

Prevention principle: When children misbehave, are insensitive to others, or do things that can hurt them—like drinking or taking drugs—don't stand in the way of consequences. Learning to live by the rules and facing the reality of consequences helps them grow into responsible, competent adults with a healthy self-esteem.

30

Putting the pieces together

In this book you have read several prevention tips for parents to help their kids avoid alcohol and drugs. I'd like to pull everything together in a sort of "preventive review" for interested parents.

- Prevention starts early. Attitudes about alcohol and drugs are formed early in life, so you'd better get your two cents' worth in with your kids while you can. Look for triggers— times when an alcohol- or drug-related happening has caught your kids' interest and use the opportunity to give them your views and accurate information.

- Give kids what they need, not always what they want. If we try to protect our kids from all the pain in life, they'll grow up without coping skills. And they'll be sitting ducks for the easy escape that alcohol and drugs offer.

- While any kid can experience alcohol and drug problems, some are at higher risk than others. Kids who have parents or other relatives with alcoholism are much more likely to become dependent on alcohol and drugs. These kids need special attention and information.

- Peer pressure is not simply a problem young people face. Everyone faces it. If parents address the problem as a "we're in this together" problem, kids are more likely to be open about the pressure they experience and more receptive to our help.

- How we (parents) behave has a great deal to do with how our kids will act. If we get drunk, drink and drive, or use drugs inappropriately, the chances are our kids will too.

- Setting rules about alcohol and drug use with significant consequences attached is very important. Letting our kids know clearly that we expect no use, and following through with consequences that "hurt" if they disobey are effective deterrents. Let kids know that this is an important issue!

- Consider a family contract which spells out exactly the standards of behavior that you expect kids to follow when it comes to alcohol and other drugs. And make sure that it is a contract which sets forth expectations for adult behavior too. (A sample family contract is on page 137.)

- Have the courage to get in touch with other parents to check out your kids' plans. Ask the necessary questions: Are the parents going to be at home for the teen party your kids are asking about? Who will transport the kids home from the upcoming school dance? An informal network of parents can be invaluable in establishing standards that everybody in your kids' group of friends can live by. Among those standards: no "taking off" or "hanging out."

- Kids see and hear high-risk messages about alcohol and drugs all the time. The messages range from "drugs get you close to people" to "drinking is a good way to cope" to "alcohol and drugs are necessary to have a good time." We can counter these messages by talking to our kids, by saying no to certain television shows, movies and concerts, by not allowing them to wear T-shirts and other items of clothing with alcohol or drug messages on them, and by becoming actively involved in our communities to change the things we see that are wrong.

- When kids are so bombarded with pro-alcohol messages, it requires extra awareness and effort on parents' part to point out to our children that alcohol also can hurt people—in small ways, such as behaviors insensitive to others' feelings, as well as in large ones, such as the tragedies of alcohol-related accidents.

- Parents can be manipulated into the trap of responding to the "if you don't entertain me, I'll probably get into drugs or alcohol just out of sheer boredom" attitude. Don't let it happen to you. Not only are you responding to pressure, and teaching them that manipulation gets them what they want, but you're not helping them develop self-sufficiency in finding their own ways to fill their time and entertain themselves.

- Kids need to be ready for the inevitable time when someone will offer them alcohol or drugs. Teaching kids ways to say no gives them important tools for that time. Help them be prepared.

- Even though we will make mistakes, we need to keep trying. Practicing prevention may get a little scary at times, but we do it in spite of our fears.

Prevention of drug and alcohol problems is made up of a bunch of little things done repeatedly over time; it doesn't happen overnight by magic. Prevention is a matter of learning, doing, and staying with it.

The reason for prevention is simple: we love our kids and we don't want to see them get hurt.

About the author

Bob Schroeder is the executive director of the Alcoholism Council of Nebraska, a statewide alcohol and drug abuse prevention agency in Lincoln, Nebraska. He is actively involved in helping communities throughout Nebraska develop their own prevention programs for youth.

He holds a master's degree in counseling psychology with a chemical dependency specialty from the University of Nebraska-Lincoln. He is a recovering alcoholic. Bob and his wife, Judy, have seven children.

Is my child using alcohol or other drugs? How can I tell?

This can sometimes be a difficult question to answer, especially during the initial stages of alcohol and drug use, when you may see little direct evidence that your child is using. Some signs of alcohol/drug use can often be confused with "normal" adolescent behavior or other health problems. Other signs, however, are very strong indicators.

We urge you not to jump to conclusions or make your own diagnosis. Nevertheless, parents should look for the following warning signs in their children's behavior, and, if patterns begin to emerge, seek further help. Answer the following fifteen questions and then refer to the scoring guide that follows:

1. Has your child's personality changed markedly? Does he/she change moods quickly, seem sullen, withdraw from the family, display sudden anger or depression, or spend hours alone in his/her room? YES _____ NO _____ UNCERTAIN _____

2. Has your child lost interest in school, school activities or school athletics? Have grades dropped at all? YES _____ NO _____ UNCERTAIN _____

3. Has your child stopped spending time with old friends? Is he/she now spending time with kids that worry you? Is your child secretive or evasive about his/her friends, and where they go and what they do? YES _____ NO _____ UNCERTAIN _____

4. Are you missing money or other objects from around the house

(money needed for alcohol and drugs), or have you noticed that your child has more money (possibly from selling drugs) than you would expect? YES _____ NO _____ UNCERTAIN _____

5.   Has your child tangled with the law in a situation involving drugs in any way? (You can be assured that if this has happened, there have been other times—probably many—when he/she has been drinking or using drugs but hasn't gotten caught.) YES _____ NO _____ UNCERTAIN _____

6.   Does your child get angry and defensive when you talk to him/her about alcohol and drugs, or refuse to discuss the topic at all? (People who are very defensive about alcohol and drugs are often hiding how much they use.) YES _____ NO _____ UNCERTAIN _____

7.   Has your child become dishonest? Do you feel you're not getting straight answers about your child's whereabouts, activities, or companions? A young person may also lie about matters that seem unrelated to alcohol or drugs. YES _____ NO _____ UNCERTAIN _____

8.   Are there physical signs of alcohol or drug use? Have you smelled alcohol on your child's breath? Have you smelled the odor of marijuana on his/her clothing or in his/her room? Slurred speech, unclear thinking, or swaggering gait are also indicators. Bloodshot eyes, dilated pupils, and imprecise eye movement may also be clues. YES _____ NO _____ UNCERTAIN _____

9.   Has your child lost interest in previously important hobbies, sports, or other activities? Has your child lost motivation, enthusiasm, and vitality? YES _____ NO _____ UNCERTAIN _____

10.   Have you seen evidence of alcohol or drugs? Have you ever found a hidden bottle, beer cans left in the car, marijuana seeds, marijuana cigarettes, cigarette rolling papers, drug paraphernalia (pipes, roach clips, stash cans, etc.), capsules, or tablets? YES _____ NO _____ UNCERTAIN _____

11.   Has your child's relationship with you or other family members deteriorated? Does your child avoid family gatherings? Is your child less interested in siblings, or does he/she now verbally

(or even physically) abuse younger brothers and sisters?
YES _____ NO _____ UNCERTAIN _____

12.   Has your child ever been caught with alcohol or drugs at school or school activities? YES _____ NO _____
UNCERTAIN _____

13.   Has your child seemed sick, fatigued, or grumpy (possibly hung over) in the morning after drug or alcohol use was possible the night before? YES _____ NO _____ UNCERTAIN _____

14.   Has your child's grooming deteriorated? Does your child dress in a way that is associated with drug or alcohol use? Does your child seem unusually interested in drug- or alcohol-related slogans, posters, music, or clothes? YES _____ NO _____
UNCERTAIN _____

15.   Has your child's physical appearance changed? Does he/she appear unhealthy, lethargic, more forgetful, or have a shorter attention span than before? YES _____ NO _____
UNCERTAIN _____

How to score the test

This questionnaire is not a scientific instrument and is *not meant to diagnose* alcohol and drug problems. It is meant to alert parents that problems are likely. The questions are "red flag" detectors and your answers may show a need for further action. Keep in mind that "yes" answers to some of these questions may simply reflect normal adolescent behavior. "Yes" answers to questions directly relating to alcohol and drug use (5, 8, 10, 12) are, of course, cause for concern; they indicate that your child is using alcohol and/or drugs, and action should be taken.

   In general, parents should look for an emerging pattern. A couple of "yes" or "uncertain" answers should alert parents to suspect alcohol and drug use, monitor the child more closely, talk to knowledgeable sources and prepare to seek help.

   If you answered "yes" to three or more questions, help is probably needed. Your child may be in the experimental stages or may already be heavily involved in alcohol and drugs. Remember, it is *very, very* difficult to handle this problem without the help of other experienced parents and/or professionals. This is *not* often a problem that passes with time; it may well be a life or death matter. If you are concerned, take action: call a knowledgeable source, your school counselor or other alcoholism/drug counselors who deal with adolescents, your local council on alcoholism or other drug/alcohol agency and discuss this questionnaire.

From the Alcoholism Council of Nebraska, Lincoln. Used by permission.

Questions for parents

Parents are powerful role models for their children. Parents who model low-risk alcohol- and other-drug-related behaviors will play a big part in reducing the chances that their children will experience problems with these substances.

Answer the questions below to help you understand the role you play in your child's experience.

Part One

_____ Yes _____ No   Does alcohol seem to be a necessary part of most or all of your social occasions?

_____ Yes _____ No   Does your child ever see you intoxicated?

_____ Yes _____ No   Do you drink to calm down or when things aren't going well?

_____ Yes _____ No   Do you ride in a car when the driver has been drinking, or do you drive after you have been drinking?

_____ Yes _____ No   Do you smoke cigarettes or chew tobacco?

_____ Yes _____ No   Do you use any illegal drugs or use prescription drugs contrary to the physician's instructions?

_____ Yes _____ No   Do you convey the attitude to your
children that teenage drinking is
acceptable?

_____ Yes _____ No   Do you convey the attitude to your
children that intoxication is sometimes
acceptable?

_____ Yes _____ No   Do you laugh about intoxicated people
rather than point out the health risks of
intoxication to your child?

_____ Yes _____ No   Do you ever involve children in your
alcohol use ("Get me a beer from the
refrigerator.")?

_____ Yes _____ No   Does your child receive conflicting
messages about alcohol and drugs at
home? (Either "alcohol is okay; drugs are
not," or parents may disagree about drug
and alcohol use.)

_____ Yes _____ No   Do you allow your child to wear clothes
with alcohol/drug pictures or slogans or
allow drug/alcohol posters in your
child's room?

_____ Yes _____ No   Do you allow your child to attend
concerts or go to movies that promote
high-risk use of alcohol or any use of
illegal drugs?

_____ Yes _____ No   Do you allow your child to associate with
kids who use alcohol or other drugs?

Part One Scoring: Yes = 1 No = 0

Part Two

_____ Yes _____ No Do you communicate with other parents to make sure your child's activities will be properly supervised and alcohol- and drug-free?

_____ Yes _____ No Do you talk to your children about alcohol or other drugs when they are exposed to pro-use messages (beer ads on TV, for example)?

_____ Yes _____ No Have you educated yourself and your children about whether or not your family is at high risk for alcohol or other drug problems? (Is there alcoholism or other drug-dependency in the family?)

_____ Yes _____ No Does your child see you model such low-risk behaviors as: "No, my limit is two per evening," "No, thanks, I'm driving," or just plain, "NO," when you are offered alcohol?

_____ Yes _____ No Have you established expectations of "no alcohol or drug use" by your children, communicated these expectations clearly, and set consequences for failure to meet these expectations? (Do you review these expectations on at least an annual basis?)

Part Two Scoring: Yes = 0 No = 1

Add your scores from Part One and Part Two.

If your score is 0: GREAT! Keep up the good work!

If your score is 1-2: Your child is growing up in a relatively low-risk environment, but you should make a concerted effort to work on those areas in which your answers scored points.

If your score is 3-4: WARNING! Your child is in an environment which may lead to potentially harmful alcohol and drug involvement.

If your score is 5 or above: Your child is growing up in a high-risk environment for alcohol or other drug problems. Changes should be made NOW! Of course, there is no certainty that your child will develop a problem, but the higher the numerical score, the greater the risk.

From the Alcoholism Council of Nebraska, Lincoln. Used by permission.

Our family's agreement on alcohol and drug use

We (I) expect you to not drink alcohol until you are of legal age or under these special circumstances:

_____

_____

_____

_____

_____

_____

When you are of legal age, if you choose to drink alcohol: drink small amounts, do not become intoxicated, and never drive.

We (I) expect you to never use illegal drugs, including marijuana.

By not honoring this agreement on alcohol and drug use, you may expect certain consequences. Some of the consequences may include:

_____

_____

_____

_____

_____

_____

If you are ever in a situation with friends or people who have been drinking, call us and we (I) will gladly come and provide a safe ride home.

In return, we (I) promise to set a good example by not drinking, or drinking small amounts, and by never using illegal drugs. We (I) will never drink on any night when you are out and may need a ride.

Signed

Parent(s)

Child

Date

From the Alcoholism Council of Nebraska, Lincoln. Used by permission.